Five Flow Self-Knowledge

Atma-Vidya Explained

Atma-Vidya of
Bhagavan Sri Ramana Maharshi

With Explanation by Nome

Published by
Society of Abidance in Truth (SAT)
1834 Ocean Street
Santa Cruz, CA 95060 USA
web: www.SATRamana.org
email: sat@satramana.org

Contents

Introduction

Atma-Vidya, Knowledge of the Self, is a concise, profound set of verses that elucidate the highest wisdom that were composed by Bhagavan Sri Ramana Maharshi. That it served as a means of spiritual instruction for his disciples and devotees is evident in the following passages found in *Talks with Sri Ramana Maharshi* (6th edition 1978):

April 2, 1937 entry 379

One Tirumalpad of Nilambur, a Malayali gentleman, asked Sri Bhagavan for an explanation of *Atma-Vidya* (Knowledge of the Self). Sri Bhagavan explained this short piece of five stanzas as follows:

Chidambaram is the famous place of pilgrimage associated with Nandanar, who sang that Atma-Vidya is most difficult of attainment. Muruganar (a longstanding devotee of Sri Bhagavan) began, however, that Atma-Vidya is the easiest of attainments. Ayye atisulabham is the burden of the song. In explanation of this extraordinary statement, he argued that Atma, being the Self, is eternally obvious even to the least of men. The original statement and the subsequent reasoning are incompatible because there need be no attainment if the Self is the substratum of all selves and so obvious, too. Naturally, he could not pursue the theme further and laid the first four lines composed by him before Sri Bhagavan for completion.

Sri Bhagavan admitted the truth of the disciple's statement and pointed out why the Self, though obvious, is yet hidden. It is the wrong identity of the Self with the body, etc.

D.: How did the wrong identity arise?

M.: Due to thoughts. If these thoughts are put an end to, the real Self should shine forth of itself.

D.: How are these thoughts to be ended?

M.: Find out their basis. All of them are strung on the single "I"-thought. Quell it; all others are quashed. Moreover, there is no use knowing all except the Self. If the Self is known, all others become known. Hence is Self-Realization the primary and sole duty of man.

D.: How to quell the "I"-thought?

M.: If its source is sought, it does not arise, and thus it is quelled.

D.: Where and how to find it?

M.: It is, in fact, the Consciousness that enables the individuals to function in different ways. Pure Consciousness is the Self. All that is required to realize the Self is to "Be Still."

D.: What can be easier than that?

M.: So, Atma-Vidya is the easiest of attainment.

April 2, 1937 entry 381

Mr. Bose, the Bengali engineer, asked the meaning of the last stanza of *Atma-Vidya (Knowledge of the Self)*. Sri Bhagavan explained on the following lines:

There is the world perceived; the perception is only apparent. It requires location for existence and light. Such existence and light are simultaneous with the rise of the mind. So, the physical existence and illumination are part of mental existence and illumination. The latter is not absolute, for the mind rises and sinks. The mind has its substratum in the Self, which is self-evident, i.e. the existence and self-luminosity are obvious. That is absolute being, continuous in sleep, waking, and dream states also.

The world consists of variety, which is the function of the mind. The mind shines by reflected light i.e., light reflected from the Self. Just as the pictures in a cinema show are seen only in diffused, i.e., artificial, light but not in a strong glare or in thick darkness, so, also, the world pictures are perceptible only in diffused, i.e., reflected light of the Self through the darkness of avidya (ignorance). The world cannot be seen either in pure ignorance, as in sleep, or in pure light, as in Self-Realization. Avidya is the cause of variety.

The engineer said that he understood it only intellectually.

M.: Because the intellect holds you at present, i.e. you are in the grip of the intellect in the waking state when you discuss these matters.

Later, it was added that Grace is needed for Realization.

The engineer asked how Grace has to be got.

M.: Grace is the Self. It is not manifest because of ignorance prevailing. With sraddha, it will become manifest. Sraddha, Grace, Light, Spirit are all synonymous with the Self.

Atma-Vidya is frequently referenced in the spiritual instruction presented at the SAT Temple. This present book is derived from five transcripts of the teachings and explanations given during five of the yearly Self-Knowledge retreats at the SAT Temple over the years. Each transcript remains distinct and whole as it is, which results in some beneficial repetition of the verses and certain aspects of the teachings. For similar reasons, questions raised by participants in these events were deleted, though the answers have been included.

The English translation of the Tamil original verses is from *The Collected Works of Ramana Maharshi,* edited by Arthur Osborne, published by Sri Ramanasramam, fourth edition 1974.

Acknowledgements

Deep appreciation and gratitude are here expressed for Sri Ramanasramam for permission to use these sacred verses, Chris Mair, Carol Johnson, and Grant Summerville for transcription of the SAT retreats presented in this book, Raman Muthukrishnan and Sangeeta Raman for proofreading and distribution of SAT publications, Raymond Teague for proofreading, Sasvati for design, layout and seeing to the printing of this book, Richard Schneider, Laura Pace and all the SAT Temple devotees whose support of the temple and the publication of these teachings of Self-Knowledge has made the present book possible.

I

Om Namo Bhagavate Sri Ramanaya

Self-Realization is abidance as the Self. That is the Self's existence as one's sole identity, without an alternative, as the Reality without other, without a second, which is without duality. Therefore, no individual becomes Self-Realized. When the imagined individuality is abandoned, the Self abides, self-revealed, comprehending itself in Self-Knowledge. The Self alone is capable of knowing itself, and, in truth, there is no other to do so. The essential practice for this Realization consists of knowledge, which, in practical application, takes the form of the inquiry summed up in the phrase, "Who am I?"

The definition of oneself as an individual, as an embodied being, is false, and, because it is false, it vanishes with inquiry to find out who you are. The real does not vanish. The real is unborn and indestructible, without beginning and end. It depends on nothing else. The ignorant belief of being defined as a bound individual depends upon unexamined delusion and has no reality apart from that delusion. In light of this, it is not truly possible or correct to speak about who realizes, who does not realize, when one realizes, and to think of oneself as, "I am not realized," "I will realize later," and such.

In order for it to be nondual, the nature of Self-Realization must be identical to the Self. Since the Realization is of the identical nature as that of the Self, it is timeless, without beginning or end, and self-luminous. The thought, "I know the Self," or, "I do not know the Self," is inapplicable. In either case, Sri Bhagavan advises inquiry into the nature of the "I" that thinks either way. "Who am I?"

Being-Consciousness-Bliss, which is the Self, innately has no bondage. The very nature of the Self is Liberation. This is something that can neither be lost nor acquired anew. If you profoundly inquire into what your nature is, the solitary Existence of the Self stands self-revealed, and the very seed of the possibility of delusion and its consequent suffering is abolished.

Sri Bhagavan bestowed this quintessential teaching concerning Self-Knowledge and the inquiry into oneself in order to realize it. Who is he? It is not quite possible to describe that, because, as the Upanishads, such as *Kathopanishad,* declare, and which is reiterated in the *Bhagavad Gita,* "Where words and thoughts turn back, unable to grasp," is his real nature.

The same One is said to exist as the Self, as God, and as the Guru. He is what he realized—the Existence of the Self—the beginningless, endless, infinite, eternal, space-like Being-Consciousness-Bliss. As for his gracious teaching, his Existence reveals itself. Existence is of the nature of infinite Consciousness.

From the position of the individual, the infinite Consciousness is referred to as "God," "the Lord of all," and such. Within the context of a dream-like illusion, yet utterly transcendent of it, this same One is said to manifest as a Sadguru, a true Guru who reveals the Truth. Sri Bhagavan said, "God, Guru, and the Self are One and the same." It is only from the perspective of a bound individual that, in the mind, one differentiates between these and considers such as three. In reality, there can be nothing other than the infinite. The infinite is formless and thus free of multiplicity. That which manifests as a form is the formless. The divinity that appears is really the divinity that is uncreated. There is really only Brahman.

Those who adhere to his teachings and are devoted to him express this devotion in terms of God and Guru. When it comes to the Self, though, it is not possible to speak anymore in these terms. If we know the Self as it is, he is, as the *Bhagavad Gita* declares, "The Self that dwells in the heart of all beings," and, as the infinite Consciousness, the Supreme, "the beginning, the middle, and the end of all beings." As the Sadguru, he brings one from the unreal to the real, from darkness to light, from death to immortality.

The question may arise, "What is the distance to be traveled between the unreal and the real?" If, in a dimly lit room, a rope appears as if it were a snake through imagination, how much transformation is required to turn that snake into a rope? How far away from your Existence are you? The Reality, which alone exists, is your very Being. Dive within, inquiring, "Who

2

am I?" Examine this existence that seems as if individualized, and you find the non-ego real Self, which has always been there and always will be there, and which is second-less.

Sri Ramana declares in the first verse:

> **Self-Knowledge is an easy thing,**
> **The easiest thing there is.**
> **The Self is something that is entirely real**
> **Even for the most ordinary man;**
> **It could be said that a clear gooseberry**
> **Is an illusion by comparison.**

Self-Knowledge is Supreme Knowledge, which is Consciousness. The Vedas declare it to be Brahman. **Self-Knowledge is the easiest thing there is.** So, for what are efforts in spiritual practice? They are only for the destruction of ignorance, the destruction of illusion. When illusion is destroyed, one realizes that nothing has been destroyed. The belief that the illusion came into existence, too, is relinquished.

Ego-death is said to be required for Self-Realization, but the ego does not actually exist. The unreal never is; the real always is. So, how can there be any difficulty in this?

Difficulties, or obstructions to Realization, encountered in spiritual practice are merely imagined. They are as unreal as the illusion that one is trying to transcend. Who is it that needs to get over illusion? Who is it that is bound? If we inquire thus, we find that there is and has been no bound individual. The individual or "I," or ego, is the root of all other delusion. If he has not been born, what can be said about the entirety of delusion? It has not actually come to be. Therefore, **Self-Knowledge is an easy thing, the easiest thing [that] there is.**

The Self is something that is entirely real even for the most ordinary man. Everyone knows that he exists. You know this without thinking about it. You know this, with or without the senses. The existence and the knowledge of it do not require sensory activity. You exist, and you know that you exist. How do you know that you exist? It is not through the senses. If the senses were to be eliminated, you would still know that you exist.

3

If you would imagine a state in which you cease to exist, you would still exist in order to have that cognition or experience. You exist always, and the knowledge of existence is innate. This is true for everyone. So, he says, **even for the most ordinary man.**

It could be said that a clear gooseberry is an illusion by comparison. The reference is to an analogy of a fruit in the palm of one's hand being so clearly obvious. There is nothing as obvious as the Self. There is nothing else as obvious as your own Existence. Everything else is known by inference or by other workings of the mind.

How can you overlook your own Existence? Your Existence is your happiness. Existence, Sat, is Chit, Consciousness, and Ananda, Bliss. Where Being is, there is Bliss. Whenever there is a limitation superimposed on happiness, which is experienced as suffering, there is an apparent overlooking of one's own existence. How can that be? Examine your experience. Do you ever cease to exist? Does happiness ever come from any place else other than the Self within? No matter what the state of your body, no matter what the state of your mind, whether you are awake, dreaming, or deep asleep, you exist, and you never cease to know of your existence.

The Truth is self-evident, evident to itself. So, Self-Knowledge is easy. It is not in the scale of easy and hard. It is easy in that the transcendent is the innate. This is not easy or difficult according to the viewpoint of the individual. Being innate, which is without the individual, it is the nature of your very Being.

If your experience is this, you understand the Maharshi well. If your experience is otherwise or is intermittent, you should ask yourself, "Why?" What do you mistake yourself to be to consider the Self to be less, obscured, or absent? What do you assume about yourself to consider Knowledge to be more or less, at any time? What do you suppose yourself to be or consider to be real to veil the infinite Bliss of your own nature?

The Maharshi says:

The Self, which shines as the Sun within the Heart,
Is real and all-pervading. It will reveal
Itself as soon as false thought is destroyed
And not one speck remains. For this thought is
The cause of the appearance of false forms,
The body and the world, which seem to be
Real things in spite of the Self, which
     steadfast stands,
The ever-changeless, firm as Truth, itself.
When the Self shines forth, darkness will be
     dispersed,
Afflictions cease, and Bliss alone remain.

The Self, which shines as the Sun within the Heart, is real and all-pervading. Your nature is pure Consciousness. Consciousness is Existence. Consciousness shines within the Heart. By "Heart" is meant the quintessence of your Being. By the term, "Heart," nothing gross or subtle is indicated; it is not a physical heart in the body and not a subtle heart in the subtle body.

How can the Self, which is spaceless and timeless, be within anything? The meaning is clear. The quintessence of your Being is Consciousness, and Consciousness is self-luminous. It does not need any other instrument or means in order to know itself. Consciousness knows itself, and nothing else illumines it. So, he says that it is like the sun.

It **is real and all-pervading.** Being real, it always is. When you know yourself, you know Reality. If you do not know your Self as you are, whatever defining idea you have of yourself is reflected in an apparently objectified universe. If you know yourself, you know Reality, and the Reality that you know is your Self. If you do not know yourself, you are merely dreaming and perceiving what is unreal. In the very place where you see what is unreal, there is actually only the Reality. In the very Heart of the one that appears to be deluded, there is only pure Consciousness, which **is real and all-pervading.** Do you ever experience anything that stands apart from the light, or knowing, of Consciousness?

Is the Existence that you are enclosed in the space of one small body? Is it restricted to the space of one mind? Though we speak of the Self as being within, "within" indicates its nonobjective nature. The idea that it is confined to a particular body should be relinquished.

Consciousness has no origin. The idea that Consciousness has its source in the mind is another figment of the mind, and it cannot be the origin of Consciousness. The idea of an origin, also, is only within the mind, a particular idea appearing in a particular state of mind referred to as waking.

Consciousness is identical with Existence, just as your experience of existing and the knowledge of existing are one and the same. They cannot be divided. You cannot separate yourself from Consciousness and see Consciousness as an object. The attempt to do so would only bring about the creation of an idea about Consciousness, but such is not the Consciousness, itself.

If you ignore your own nature and consider yourself as an individual, who does not really exist, and correspondingly consider Consciousness, or the Self, as an object, even though it is always nonobjective, you can think that you cannot see it and cannot find it. If that misidentification is done away with by inquiry, it is obvious that you cannot lose it.

What you possess you can lose; what you are you cannot lose. If you acquire or attain it, it will be lost. What comes goes; what appears disappears; what arises sets. It requires only a mere change of a state of mind, for the knowledge of the previous state to disappear, such as when you fall asleep. Consciousness' Knowledge of itself is not like that. Self-Realization does not occur in any of the states of mind. Can the recognition that there are no states of mind actually occur in a state of mind? When you discriminate between Consciousness and thinking, can that discrimination be composed of thought? When you succeed in discriminating between Consciousness and thought, is that discerning wisdom a thought or something more formless? The formless is not contained within a state. To say the practice occurs within a given state, such as the waking state, is alright as an explanation to show where the emphasis in spiritual practice should be applied, lest the aspirant be concerned about meditation in the dream state or meditation in deep sleep. If meditation is inquiry into your own nature, the entire practice does not occur on the mental level. The practice cannot be said to occur within a state of mind, because it is the very nature of the practice to bring about transcendence of the states of mind. How would it be possible for that to occur, if the practice were restricted to a state of mind? The practice does not occur by anything concerning the five sheaths. Otherwise, how would it be possible to hop over those sheaths to get to the real Self? The power to know your Self belongs only to the Self. It is only expedient teaching that describes practice as occurring by the vijnanamaya-kosa in order to indicate the Self's absolute transcendence even of ignorance and knowledge.

You exist, whether the mind is awake, dreaming, or asleep. The Existence is invariable. If it were a product of those states, it would change when those states change, but that is not the experience of anyone. The Existence is identical with Consciousness, and Consciousness alone constitutes the Knowledge. If you deeply inquire to know yourself, is the substance of this direct experience a mental recognition? If there would be a mental recognition, it would be mere ornamentation and redundant, would it not?

Confusion comes from the misidentification of the Self with thought, particularly the thought of "I," the vague assumption of being an individual who goes in and out of a state and who expects the knowledge to be a change in some thought-constituted manner. The Knowledge, though, is not thought, and the Self is not the individual. As soon as the misidentification is done away with, the confusion is over, and nothing, real or unreal, has changed its nature.

The world is concomitant with the "I." They rise and fall together. The "I" that comes and goes, the "I" that corresponds to the idea, "I will cease," is not your actual Existence. Your real Existence does not cease. If you suppose that you are not, you are still there to know you are not. The identification with everything that corresponds to a "you" that can come and go should be abandoned. This abandonment is Knowledge.

It will reveal itself as soon as false thought is destroyed and not one speck remains.

False thought ought to be destroyed. What is false thought? There are two ways to understand the phrase, "false thought," both of which are correct, neither of which is false.

The first pertains to those thoughts that constitute the forms of ignorance. Such ideas as, "The world is real," "I am the body," all attachments, which are erroneous thoughts about the place of happiness, and all kinds of binding thoughts should be destroyed. If they are destroyed, the naturally free state of the Self is revealed.

The second way of understanding "false" is as an adjective that describes the nature of thought. All thought is false. In reality, there is Consciousness, which is without differentiation. A thought is the concept of some differentiation in Consciousness. It is said to arise after the first differentiation, which is the notion "I," and all the thoughts become the objects of that "I," but the truth is that the one indivisible Consciousness is the one reality. It is not and cannot be differentiated. It cannot be divided into subject and object, "I" and "this."

How is false thought to be destroyed? The unreal seems to be real, only because of one's belief in it. The belief in it makes it seem as if real, which is a testimony to the power of Reality and the strength of faith. Belief can make the unreal appear real, and one minute spark of the power of the real Self can make an entire unreal world seem as if solid and expansive. If the false is known as false, it disappears. It survives only because of belief in it. It is a superimposition of illusion upon the reality. The moment you know the unreal as unreal, the moment you know ignorance as ignorance, as not being true at all, ignorance ceases to exist and cannot arise again. Ignorance persists only because of belief in it. Belief gives ignorance a sense of continuity, as well as a sense of validity. Without validity and without continuity, how will ignorance remain? Ignorance is self-generated. If you do not generate it, who will? How is false thought destroyed? It is destroyed by the knowledge that it is false. Inquire to determine "What is real?" "Who am I?" The ignorant thoughts are destroyed. The very idea that there is an existent mind, an existent thought, is destroyed.

If a person has attachment to something in the world, it is due to a misconception regarding the source of happiness.

Because of the misconception regarding the source of happiness, there are limitations to that experience, and, therefore, there is suffering. To put an end to the suffering, all the person needs to know is the real source of happiness. Once the source is interiorly ascertained to be within, the attachment is gone from that moment forward, and, where there is no attachment, there is no possibility of a person suffering in this world or due to anything in this world. What has just been said about happiness applies to every attachment, every misidentification, and any form of ignorance.

And not one speck remains. The objective portion of the mind should be relinquished. The supposed subject, the "I" notion, should also be abandoned. This ego is the final speck. It is not self-existent, and its appearance is only imaginary.

You have this hijacker pretending to be a chauffeur driving the car of your mind. The ego works only when hired to do so. Who is hiring the ego-driver? Why are you hiring this impostor? If you say that you know that happiness is within but feel compelled to follow craving, you do not really know, do you? You may have an idea about it, which is in the right direction, but such is not actual knowledge. When you actually know something is suffering, you do not go near it. Of course, it is not things that cause you to suffer, but only illusions in your mind. Nothing will be able to compel you to go toward an illusion in your mind, once you know that it is an illusion.

You know that you are not a donkey. Is there anything that could compel you, in any situation, to take up the belief that you are a donkey? It just could not happen. You could not become a donkey even if you wanted to. It just could not happen, because you know, beyond a shadow of a doubt, that you are not a donkey. You are a human being. After having inquired, in Self-Knowledge, you can no more believe that your happiness is outside, or that you are the body, or that you are an individual than you can believe presently in the assertion that you are a donkey. You just simply are not one, and you know it. For you to know it, you do not need to be continuously thinking, "I am not a donkey." It is only if someone or something presents the idea, the false impression, "We have doubts; we think you are a donkey," that you say, "I am not one." If not, however, you do not even need to think about it. It is just absurd. It is the same with every bit of ignorance. Any question regarding speech and action is like asking why you are braying and walking around in the stall? You are not a donkey to begin with. If you know that you were not a donkey, the possibilities of such occurring are no longer there. Nothing is compelling you, other than your own belief of being a donkey, and that is a testimony, not to your "donkey-hood," but to the power of belief.

You cannot possibly be a donkey. In the same way, you cannot possibly be an embodied ego, and the activities attributed to the ego are like the activities attributed to the donkey. Have deep, true Knowledge. When you really know where happiness is, you revel in it because it is your nature to be happy—Ananda enjoying itself. You do not intentionally suffer. No one tries to suffer; everyone tries to be happy, because happiness is the nature of all. Suffering is due only to inverted or mistaken attempts to be happy.

Once you know where happiness is, you do not become attached to anything in this world. Once you really know you are not the body, the freedom of this is so great that nothing is able to convince you to resume the delusion of embodiment again. Similar is the case with every aspect of ignorance.

Merely to learn the words or the corresponding thoughts that pertain to the teaching of Sri Bhagavan or Advaita Vedanta, while such may be good, is not the Knowledge that is lauded and taught. The Knowledge is always experiential, that which you know or feel to be real. To really know, inquire.

Inquiry is primarily to find out who you are. When dealing with particular tendencies, which have their continuity and power only from you, it is worthwhile to ask, "Why?" The answer to that question cannot possibly be anything of an external nature. By "Why?" is meant tracing the particular tendency to the various false definitions or misidentifications that are its root. The definitions pertain to "me." "Who am I?"

The moment you turn your mind inward to inquire in this manner, already you are disidentified, because, by your very intention to examine it, you have ceased to regard the ignorance as being of your nature, and it has become something objective to you, of which you are going to divest yourself. For the person who is endowed with an intense desire for Liberation, who is desirous of inquiring, at the moment the desire to inquire arises, the freedom has already begun.

Inquiry does not belong to the individual, but it dissolves the individual, and it is never an action; it is always Knowledge. Thus, Adi Sankara's instruction in *Atma Bodha* that action does not bring Liberation; Knowledge alone is Liberation. The body, speech, and mind, and their activities, are not in conflict with ignorance, but Knowledge destroys ignorance, just as light destroys darkness.

It is not a necessity to do hard labor to drain the waters of a mirage. You do, though, need to know that it is a mirage. When you know it is a mirage, you do not run after it to quench your thirst.

All of this appears subtle, or even mysterious, until you actually inquire. Then, what is true is self-evident, and what is false is obviously so.

Where neither the thought of "I" nor of anything else survives, that is the Knowledge that there is only this one Self that is the Reality. There is the Liberation from the imagined bondage.

The depth of experience is determined by the diminishing of the ego and its corresponding ideas. The Self will reveal itself to itself, all by itself, without an "other," **as soon as false thought is destroyed and not one speck remains.** Is there a speck of illusion that you want to retain? The destruction of the manifested tendencies leads to the destruction of the central notion of an ego, and the destruction of the central notion of an ego leads to the obliteration of the tendencies that depend upon it. The depth of any experience is always found in the Knowledge-essence, which corresponds to the dissolution of the ego. The ego is ignorance. Where there is Knowledge, ignorance is not, just as, where there is light, there is not darkness.

Remove from any spiritual experience the ego dissolution aspect, or the Knowledge-essence, and what remains of it? No matter how the approach is made, no matter what kind of spiritual practice, it is the Knowledge-essence that is the living part of it, and it is the dissolution of the ego in any of its forms that correlates to the depth of the experience.

For this thought is the cause of the appearance of false forms, the body and the world, which seem to be real things in spite of the Self, which steadfast stands, the ever-changeless, firm as Truth, itself.

The false forms are created only in thought. The entire world is merely in the mind. **The body and the world are the false forms.**

From the position of a body, one apparently perceives the forms of the world, just as, in last night's dream, from the position of the dream body, you experienced a dream world. The character endowed with a dream body and the dream world are both unreal. The only thing real in the dream experience is the Consciousness that illuminates all, that knows all, but Consciousness has no form within the dream. It is the only real thing there, yet it cannot be perceived there. It is not part of the dream world, yet it could be said to pervade the dream world entirely. Likewise is it with the dream body. The waking state perceptions or experiences are very similar to the dream experiences.

How do the body and the world appear in a dream? You think, and the thought appears to be solid due to the power of your own reality, though there is nothing solid in the dream at all. So it is in the present waking state. The experiences of the forms of the world and the body seem as if real. From where does this sense of reality come? The forms are changeful. The experience, "This is real," seems to be present. From where does this feeling, "This is real," come? It cannot come from the forms. The forms of the world do not say, "We exist!" Likewise, the body does not say, "I exist!" Someone who is not the body and who is not of the world has this feeling, "This is. This exists." The source of the sense of reality is the perceiver of it. What is the nature of the perceiver? Is he a body or anything of the world? Can he be conceived in thought? He is, as the Upanishad proclaims, "the unknown Knower of all that is known."

The known is the body and the world, the false forms, **which seem to be real things in spite of the Self, which steadfast stands.** Everything in the world changes. Your body changes. Everything conceived in thought changes. It changes as your mind changes states, such as waking and dreaming.

Does your existence change? How can the combination of the changeful and the changeless be possible, except through delusion, thinking that the body is "I"? Except through mere imagination, how can you say of the world, "This is. This is real."

Even in the midst of delusion, the Self shines, **steadfast,** unmoving, and utterly unalterable. In the entirety of illusion, there is no alteration of the Self's nature. The Self never becomes less, stained, bound, or impure. In its unborn nature, it is as it is for all eternity, **the ever-changeless, firm as Truth itself.**

Reality does not become unreal at any time. The unreal does not become real at any time. There is no crossing over from the unreal, or illusion, which has no existence, into the real, which is ever-existent. Conversely, there is no changing of the real Self into anything that it is not, the unreal. The Self can never be the not-Self, and the not-Self can never be or become the Self. The body, the embodied, and the things of the world never become the reality. The Reality is never transformed into those things. The real ever is; the unreal never is; the Self remains steadfast. It is steadfast in relation to things moving, but the essence of the steadfastness is its solitary existence. It is undivided, and there is nothing other than itself to affect it. It does not change itself; it will not change its own nature. It is the Truth, itself.

The forms of the world are just thought. The body is included in this. Changeful, fleeting, unreal thought does not change the Reality of the Self. No matter how much is thought of with the mind, the Self remains just as it is, no more, no less. The space of infinite Consciousness, which is the Self of real Being, is not affected. This is said in relation to the movement of thought. Transcendent of that perspective, it just is as it is. The heart of steadfastness is the solitary Existence of the real Self, the One without a second. In the context of many, we may say that it is the unchanging One, but really it is the only One.

He concludes the verse with:

When the Self shines forth, darkness will be dispersed, afflictions cease, and Bliss alone remain.

That Self always shines. By its light, even ignorance is discerned. The shadows are there only because of the light, and the light, itself, is shadow-less. The light that cannot be extinguished we say shines forth when the obscuring ignorance is destroyed. When you cease to think of "I" and "this," when the conception, or assumption, of existing as an ego-entity with a body in a world is relinquished, when such imagination ceases, the Self shines in its own light. There was no moment when it did not shine. While practicing, one may say, "When will I be wise? When will I be liberated?" The sages say, "When have I been bound? When was I not liberated?"

When the Self shines forth, darkness will be dispersed: As phrased in this manner, the causality is the Self shines forth, and darkness is dispersed. The power of that dispersal is the same shining Self, so that the end appears as the means. The Self, which is pure Knowledge, appears as the power of inquiry. The Self, which is infinite and eternal, appears as the desire for Liberation, which goads one to intense, earnest spiritual practice.

What happens then? **Afflictions cease, and Bliss alone remain[s].** Why do afflictions cease? They cease because Bliss is your Being, and, when the knowledge of Being is clarified, the knowledge, or experience, of Bliss is unobstructed. Wherever Being is, there is Bliss. Is there a time when you are not? Then, there is no time when you are away from happiness. If your experience seems contrary, ask yourself, "Why?" You will find that it is due only to misidentification. Inquire, "Who am I?" Discovering Being, you discover Bliss. As Being is without a cause, so happiness is without a cause. As Being-Consciousness is without condition or limit, so Bliss is without limit or condition. This being the case, there has never been a good reason to be unhappy, because there has never been a time when you were other than the real Self.

When one inquires and arrives at such Knowledge, the Bliss of one's nature shines naturally without any obstruction. The idea of losing it becomes impossible. As there is nothing in life or death that can put an end to Being, there is nothing in life or death that can put an end to Bliss. It is the nature of the experiencer. The same Bliss is said to shine as love, as peace, as joy, and as the feeling of being free.

> **The thought "I am the body" is the string**
> **On which are threaded diverse thoughts like beads.**
> **Therefore, on diving deep upon the quest**
> **"Who am I and from where (whence)?" thoughts**
>   **disappear,**
> **And Consciousness of the Self then flashes forth**
> **As the "I-I" within the cavity**
> **Of every seeker's Heart. And this is Heaven,**
> **This is that Stillness, the abode of Bliss.**

The thought "I am the body" is the string on which are threaded diverse thoughts like beads. The notion "I" is integrally connected with the idea of everything else. Every idea about the world depends upon the idea "I am the body." If there is the misconception "I am the body," which is not true, you think that you are limited to the scope of it, that you are born when it is born, you grow when it grows, you decay when it is decays, you die when it dies, and you think you are in a world, although it would be more appropriate to say that the world and the body are in you, rather than you are in them.

Upon this notion, "I am the body," are threaded all of the pseudo-experiences, or conceptions, of "this." If the body is subtle, the conceptions of "this" are subtle. If the body is gross, the conceptions of "this" similarly are gross. The "I am the body" conception is pivotal to delusion. The granthi, or knot, is the conception that ties together Consciousness and the body, the Self and the body, the Consciousness with the inert. If the knot is cut, delusion crumbles. Dissolve the form of the experiencer, and the limited experiences that are based upon the form of the experiencer correspondingly are destroyed, leaving the vast expanse of Being-Consciousness-Bliss, the real Existence. Destroy the illusion by Knowledge. The remainder, naturally present, is the Truth.

Therefore, on diving deep How do you dive deep? You dive deep by the quest "Who am I?" and "From where, or whence, am I?" "From where does this notion 'I' come?" Does it come from your body? You say, "my body." The "my" refers to someone who is other than the body. The one who is regarded as the owner is someone other than the body. Who is this? Where does the sense of "I" originate? It does not come from the body; it does not come from any of the parts of the body, such as the head, the torso, and the limbs. Where does the sense of "I" arise? Trace inwardly, "From where is 'I'?"

The "I" cannot be the body. The "I" that says "my body," cannot be the body. Then, no one else is their bodies, so how will we distinguish among the supposed individuals?

The "I am the body" conception gives rise to the sense of being located in time and space. "I am here and now" is imagined from the misidentified perspective. If you are not the body, where are you? If you are not the body, what is the nature of everyone? Everyone is no longer a multiplicity. If you are not the body, where do you begin and where does somebody else begin? Where do you end? Do you end in time or in space? These do not apply to the Self.

"Who am I? From where am I?" If you inquire in this way, **thoughts disappear, and [the] Consciousness of the Self then flashes forth.** If there is no form of "I," there is no form of anything else. The "this," is always a mirror image of the "I." However the "I" is conceived, so is "this" conceived. Although we may speak of it as perceived, it really is just in the mind, as in a dream. If the "I" has a form—"I" am the body—"this" will have a form, There is the "world." If I am not the body, what is "this"? Without the forms of "I" and "this," what is thought?

You may be accustomed to the interweaving of streams of thoughts appearing as interior conceptions and external perceptions, but there is something else that is more familiar to you, and you have never quite become thoroughly adapted or accustomed to those streams of thought. Otherwise, you would not seek to be free of them. They are familiar because they tend to be repetitive. If not the actual form of a thought, the manner in which the thinking proceeds is repetitive. Samsara is characterized by repetition, the wise say. It is repetition within one's mind, rebirth after rebirth of the same conception, the same erroneous definitions. If you trace for whom these streams are and comprehend his nature, you find innate freedom from, the innate transcendence of, those streams. If you trace for whom these thoughts are—"Who am I?"—the false definitions about the "I," which give rise to those streams of thought, without which those streams of thought cannot appear or survive, ceases.

The "I" appears as a thought, but you are not a thought. You exist with or without thought. The thought of "I" is one thing; the Existence that is really I is another. Trace all the threads of thought to the notion "I." Then, inquire "Who am I?" There is no place from which those streams originate, but, as long as you do not inquire, the streams seem to be going on in a dream that is ages old. The streams of thought about everything are based on the definitions of you. The definitions of you are woven into all of the patterns of thinking, and the definitions have one supposition at their core—"I." Without it, there is no creation. What is regarded as the entire universe is your Self, but where and when the "I" arises, there and then begins division.

That which inspires you to seek the Reality must be something that exists irrespective of the presence or absence of thought. True Knowledge does not have much to do with thought, nor is it the suppression of thought. It is not necessarily an interruption of thought at the level of thought. The destruction of thought is the abandonment of the very idea that thought is ever existent. If one merely stops thought, as beneficial as that might be, depending upon the spiritual circumstances, it will resume. Thought ceases at times, such as deep dreamless sleep and similar states, but we do not see any permanent Liberation coming from that break, even if one has had that many times.

Where "me" and "mine" vanish, something else arises and shines that is true and real. It has nothing to do with thought. If you maintain the idea "my thoughts," it will not shine for you. If you retain the idea "my absence of thought," it will not shine for you. Where the "me" and the "mine" disappear, it shines. Emphasis is placed on Self-Knowledge and not just the stoppage of thought. The Self and its Realization are not dependent upon the stoppage of thought. The Self is thought-transcendent and so is its Realization.

The thoughts are completely inert and have no knowing power. A thought does not declare its own existence. Something else knows it. So much is this so that, apart from the something else that knows, the thought cannot be said to exist at all. Have you ever known or experienced a thought apart from the Consciousness that knows it? If it has no independent existence, it does not actually have any existence.

If you become entangled in thoughts, you are naturally going to have a yearning to be free of them. The yearning must come from something that knows better and that already stands beyond thought. If the yearning turns in on itself, which is the practice of inquiry, thought becomes irrelevant.

Surrender and inquiry signify the dissolution of the notion of "I." If you inquire as to who you are, your experience will be abidance just as Sri Bhagavan, and, if you surrender to Sri Bhagavan, he takes over everything, and there is nothing left for you, neither you nor yours. "I" and "mine" disappear entirely in either case.

The inquiry should be addressed regarding identity. You need not worry about whether the thoughts appear or not. Just address the assumption of "I"—"me" and "mine." The illusory presence of "me" and "mine" makes bondage; the absence of "me" and "mine" makes for Liberation. If there is no "me," there is no start for the thoughts; if there is no "mine," there is no possessor of the thoughts.

Therefore, on diving deep upon the quest "Who am I and from where (whence)?" thoughts disappear, and Consciousness of [the] Self then flashes forth as the "I-I" within the cavity of every seeker's Heart.

Inquiring "Who am I?" you lose the misidentifications. Inquiring, "Whence am I?" the sense of "I" returns to its origin, its rightful place, free of superimposition. What is the result? The Consciousness, the pure Knowledge of the Self, which is the Knowledge that is Consciousness, **flashes forth** to itself, because there is none other to whom it would flash, the false identity having been dissolved. The only thing that remains of "I" is Consciousness, said to be flashing forth to itself.

This **flashes forth as the "I-I,"** which is the continuous identification with pure Existence, just the Self. It is not as an ego-"I," but is that which is truly "I," **within the cavity of every seeker's Heart.** That is the space of quintessential Being, which is the space of Consciousness.

And this is Heaven, this is that Stillness, the abode of Bliss. This is Heaven within. Where else is Heaven to be found? It **is that Stillness.** What is stillness? It is the same as Silence, the unmoving, invariable Existence. It is the Maharshi's silence; it is Dakshinamurti's silence; it is the stillness of the unmoving Brahman, which never becomes other than what it is, the immutable One. The immutable One, the real Stillness, transcendent Silence is the abode of Bliss. One who abides in That exists as That. So, you live in Heaven; you are Heaven. Being still, you are the Stillness, the Silence. Similarly, when you know the Abode of Bliss, you are the state or Abode of Bliss, and, being That, you cannot lose it. What you go into, you may come out of, but the true Heaven is That which you are, and it is neither lost nor gained.

> **What is the use of knowing everything**
> **Except the Self? What else is there to know**
> **For anyone when the Self, itself, is known?**
> **On realizing in oneself the Self,**
> **Which is the only self-effulgent One**
> **In myriads of selves, the Light of the Self**
> **Will clearly shine within. This is, indeed,**
> **The true display of Grace, the ego's death,**
> **And the unfolding of the Bliss supreme.**

What is the use of knowing everything except the Self? Since the conception of yourself goes into the make-up of knowing anything else, if you do not know yourself, what is it that you know in the guise of knowing "this?" You know nothing more than the reflections of your own false definitions.

First, within is to be found happiness. If you do not know yourself, but you know anything else, you do not find the happiness for which you yearn. The same holds true for peace. Secondly, what is the use of knowing everything else that comes and goes, without knowing you who remain? Thirdly, what is the use of knowing anything else, which does not actually exist as that, without knowing the real Existence, which is your Self?

What else is there to know for anyone when the Self, itself, is known?

Of spiritual Knowledge, the finality, which is the Vedanta, the final, highest Knowledge, is Knowledge of one's Self. All other kinds of spiritual knowledge lead one only to the point of inquiring to know one's Self. In the end, you must know yourself. That known, there is completion, there is satisfaction, and there is no further distance to travel.

Anything **else** is an unreal reflection of ignorance regarding yourself, but, if, free of the world and body forms, you do know yourself, free of the misconception of being an individual entity, what else is there to know? There is no second knower as the mind or ego, and there is nothing else, nothing other, to know. There is something other, as long as you assume that you are an individual and as long as you maintain the "I am the body" misconception. If the "I am the body" misconception is gone, what is other? There is no other. If the very basic notion of "I" is gone, there is no "this." There is, therefore, nothing else to be known.

If you are born, there is some creation to know. If you are unborn, there is no creation.

As long as you consider yourself as in a dream—the dream character appearing as a dream body—there are dream others. When you wake up from the dream, what happens? You abandon the idea that the dream world is real or existing, and, most importantly, you abandon the identity of being the dreamer, the dreaming character. After you wake up from a dream, what happens to all of the other dream creatures? Where do they go? As separate individuals, they are not. They have been resolved into their essence, which is you.

The body and the world external to it are just thought forms. There is nothing to them but the thought of them, which is why they appear only in one state of mind according to that state. The state of mind composes the forms of that state. It not only creates them, but it is the stuff of which they are made. The waking state of mind composes the world and bodies that you apparently experience, just like a dreaming state of mind makes up the substance of the dream. Just as the body and the world have no existence apart from the thought, the thought has no existence apart from the Self that knows it. For the unborn, there is no creation.

On realizing in oneself the Self, which is the only Self-effulgent One, in myriads of selves

What is reality? What can be more practical than knowing Existence as it is? The highest is actually the most practical. If the Self, or Existence, is unchanging, as everyone intuitively knows it to be, yet one thinks that the world arises from the Self, the question is how could something arise in that which is unchanging? What would cause such a change to occur in that which is changeless? The difference between the world of changeful things and the Self is the difference between the unreal and the real, between the snake and the rope.

What is the everyday reality that we experience? It depends on how you define the "we." According to one definition, the "we" is day-to-day in the world. Without such definition, the "we" is only the Self, and the eternal is the day by day. If you say that there is a real, unchanging Existence, and there is also a changeful part, either you have a dualism to resolve, or you do not really know, in the depths, what is real. If, in the same breath, you say, "I know myself, yet I see the world," is that "I" the same "I" that is the Self, or is it a different one? If it is two, how do we become two?

Existence does not rise and set. How can that which does not rise and set give rise to anything else? How would the undivided become divided, the changeless become changeful? Instructions are given, such as, "The world rises and sets in the Self." The emphasis is on the Self. It is not for us to build up an idea, "This thought, 'The world is in the Self,' is the finality." It is said only to wean one from the more ignorant idea that the world exists independent of the Self.

"All is Brahman." "The world, regarded as the Self, does exist or is real." What is meant by "the world, regarded as the Self"? It cannot be merely intellectually renaming the world, "the Self." Some deeper experience is indicated, in which that which you previously referred to as the world is found to be only the homogeneous Existence. The snake is found only to be the rope.

It is like saying, "Apart from the rope, there is no snake," or, "The snake appears only on the rope." It does not mean the rope actually changed into a snake, or a snake arises in a rope. The meaning is that the rope alone is there, and the snake is not there at all. What you think to be a snake is really just the existence of the rope. So it is with the Self, which is Existence, and the supposed experience of the world.

On realizing in oneself the Self means one's identity is just the Self. The Realization occurs within. What is within? It is not within the body. It is not within the domain of thought. The real within-ness realizes its own nature, the Self within oneself, **which is the only self-effulgent One in myriads of selves:** From the perspective of misidentification with the body, there seems to be an individualized consciousness, so that one consciousness knows one thing, and another consciousness knows another thing. That is said to be the mind, which may be regarded as a combination of Consciousness and the body.

The only self-effulgent One in myriads of selves: Thinking of myriads of selves, where there is only one Self, is akin to seeing numerous suns in shallow pools of water. In a hundred shallow pools of water, you would see a hundred suns. Of course, you know that you are looking only at the reflection. This is the equivalent of looking at the minds considered in relation to the bodies. The light in them is actually only one light. The reflections have no self-luminosity. So it is with the mind apparently inhabiting a body.

Make your vision nonobjective, and lift it from the reflecting medium, the mind, the senses, and the body, to the source, which is all light, pure Consciousness. If you realize the Self as yourself, the undifferentiated Self, in which multiplicity is impossible, the Light of the Self clearly shines. Where does it shine? It shines within, just for itself. Self-Knowledge is for the Self, of the Self, by the Self—all being one and the same Self. It is not the knowing of anything else. This has already been negated in the preceding lines.

Know your Self as the infinite, homogeneous Consciousness. If you mix it up with the senses and with the mind, which cognizes the senses and contains the senses within it, there are other things to know. Then, there are other people defined in terms of bodies, and there are other things, which are said to constitute the world. Remove the definitions from the seer, and what is seen? Trace the light from the reflections to the source. Cease to define the knower in terms of the known, and what is his real nature?

This is, indeed, the true display of Grace, the ego's death. The ego has no part in this. The ego does not inquire; it never occurs to the ego to inquire. The ego is not really a sentient entity to do any such thing. It is not a separate knowing entity; it is but an illusion.

If the ego dies, all is right. Its death is the discovery of its nonexistence. We may consider grace to be responsible for everything wonderful that happens. We can further regard Grace to be responsible for everything that happens, whether we think it is wonderful or not. Sri Bhagavan says, **This,** the revelation of Reality to itself, **is the true display of Grace.** The supreme Grace is none other than the Realization of the Self, and it is **the unfolding of the Bliss supreme.**

If you know your Self, there remains nothing else to be known. Experiencing the Self, there remains nothing else to be experienced, and the happiness of the Self leaves no other happiness to be desired. Sri Bhagavan reveals supreme bliss, supreme peace. There is nothing beyond it. If one conceives of something beyond it, one has not yet experienced it. Whoever experiences what he describes is swallowed and absorbed, and what has been fully absorbed does not arise again.

> **In order that the bonds of destiny**
> **And all its kindred may at last be loosed,**
> **And so that one may also be released**
> **From the dread cycle of both birth and death,**
> **This path than others is far easier;**
> **Therefore, be still and keep a silent hold**
> **On tongue and mind and body. That which is**
> **The self-effulgent will arise within.**
> **This is the Supreme Experience. Fear will cease.**
> **This is the boundless sea of perfect Bliss.**

Breaking the bondage of **destiny.** In the sastras, destiny is described as being composed by one's own efforts, that is, one's own karma. The supreme Lord is regarded as the distributor of the fruits of the karma. Such is referred to as destiny. Karma is the action and the reaction to it. Actions are performed with the body, speech, and mind. The reactions are experienced by the same three.

So that one may also be released from the dread cycle of both birth and death This is the samsara. For that which has birth, death is certain; for that which has death, birth is certain. This is declared in the *Bhagavad Gita*. Find that in you which has neither birth nor death. An "I" arises and falls; it cannot be you. A body is born and dies; it cannot be you. Within, find that which did not ever begin and which cannot possibly end, and regard that alone as yourself. For that, there is no karma or destiny, or its results or its attributes. This is the direct path.

This path than others is far easier. He has already stated that Realization is the easiest thing there is. Now, he states the path that is the easiest, which is the most direct. **Therefore, be still and keep a silent hold on tongue and mind and body.** What is the stillness? He has addressed the tongue, which refers to speech, the body, and the mind. Thoughts are said to constitute the mind. Stillness is more than being without thought; it is something deeper.

Be still: do not swerve from your identity; do not move from the Self. The movement from the Self is only imagination. Once imagining, you seem to travel far and wide. Really, you go nowhere. Do not move from the Knowledge of your essential nature, **and keep a silent hold on tongue and mind and body.** What is the silent hold? It is not just keeping quiet and refraining from speaking. How do you keep a silent hold on the body and the mind? Where the false identification as a separate individual vanishes, there is Silence. Silence is that state in which no "I" arises. Keep an egoless hold on the body, mind, and speech. Do not make these forms of the ego. Do not manifest the ego through these. Remain "I"-less and do not have egotism in relation to them.

Inquire. Once inquiring, do not move from the Knowledge of yourself, and be silent, that is, "I"-less in relation to the mind, speech, and body. Body here refers to all kinds of activities, as well as the body, itself. Speech may be applied to all kinds of relating as well as the actual speaking. Similarly, the mind refers to intellect, mind, and thought in all its permutations.

That which is the self-effulgent will arise within. It will shine in its own essential Existence. **This is the Supreme Experience. Fear will cease.** Why does fear cease? Why does fear arise? The Upanishad says, "Where there is a second, there is fear." The implication is that where there is no second, no duality, there is no fear. In one of his bhashyas, Sri Sankara states that no one is afraid of himself. You can be afraid only of another; you cannot be afraid of yourself.

The Supreme Experience is that in which there is no subject and object, no experiencer experiencing an object of experience. The Supreme Experience is just undivided Existence as it is. For that, there is no fear because there is no other, there is no second.

When you have fear, it is because you assume that something that might occur will take away your happiness or remove or diminish your existence in some way. No one wants happiness to disappear, and no one wants existence to cease. Indeed, they do not want their existence to cease because they intuit that happiness and existence are identical. If you know yourself as Existence and are reveling in your own Bliss, which is without condition and without cause, how will you be afraid? Without duality, without misconception about happiness, without misconception about your Existence, such is the Supreme Experience, the boundless sea of perfect Bliss, and, in that, fear ceases.

It is impossible for God to be afraid. Of what would God be afraid? If the "I" has no existence apart from God, what would God, or I, fear? It is unimaginable that God would have fear. The very idea of "I" is as something more powerful than God that could break off from God, divide God, whether existing in God, alongside of God, or outside God. But nothing is more powerful than God. As for the universe, how does God see God? With God's Eye what is seen?

Imagine you stand apart from God as "I," and all kinds of troubles arise, as many as you imagine, and all of them are based on the single conception that you exist as an individual entity, that God is somehow not fully God. If God is really infinite, all pervading, omniscient, omnipotent, omnipresent, etc., that does not leave any room for you, other than God. Then, you cannot claim anything as your own—"my mind, my thoughts, my body, my world, my perceptions," and so forth and so on. Surrender becomes the absorption in the Knowledge that God alone is. That is the same doubtless state as the Realization that the Self alone is.

> **Annamalai, the Transcendental One,**
> **That is the Eye behind the eye of the mind,**
> **Which eye and other senses cognizes,**
> **Which in their turn illuminate the sky (space)**
> **And all the other elements as well,**
> **That is again the Spirit-sky (space) in which**
> **The mind-sky (space) does appear; That**
>   **shines within**
> **The Heart which is of every thought quite free**
> **And with gaze fixed within remains fixed as That;**
> **Annamalai (Arunachala), the self-effulgent, shines.**
> **But Grace is needed most. So, faithful be**
> **Unto the Self and Bliss will then result.**

The Maharshi equates Arunachala with the Supreme Self, the unmoving One. How can there be motion in the unmoving One? It is transcendental. It is absolute, unrelated to anything else, the solitary Existence before the idea of anything else ever comes to be.

That is the Eye behind the eye of the mind, which eye and other senses cognizes. What do you know of anything, other than your sense perceptions of it? What do you know of your sense perceptions, other than your thoughts, or mental cognitions, of the same? You know nothing of the objects seen except the seeing, of the objects heard except the hearing, and likewise with all of the senses and percepts. You have never experienced a sense object apart from the sensing of it. The sensing is inert and is known by the mind. You have never known a sensation apart from the mind which cognizes. The world is in the senses; the senses are in the mind. In delusion, one thinks that it is the other way around, the mind is in a body with the senses, and the body and senses are within the world. The actual experience, though, is that the entire world is within the context of the senses, and the senses are only in the mind. What knows the mind? If you trace inwardly, the identity, the knowing, and the reality return to their rightful place, and the inverted view of delusion is over.

which in their turn illuminate the sky (space) and all the other elements, as well, that is again the Spirit-sky (space) in which the mind-sky (space) does appear. Your mind moves. Where does it move? It can move about all day, for a lifetime, for a kalpa (a thousand ages), or longer. With all of that motion, where does it move? From where to where?

The entire space of the universe is contained within the space of your mind. If you think of the mind as being embodied, how this is so seems incomprehensible. If you do not hold such conceptual limitations, how the universe is within the mind is easily ascertainable. In what space is your mind contained? The mind is contained within the great space of infinite Consciousness. The infinite space of Consciousness, the space-like Existence, is your nature. When the mind moves, it traverses no distance. Going outward and inward is mentioned just by way of instruction. Really, there is no such thing as outward, and inward is the infinite space-like Consciousness and not a place.

The knowledge of all things is just the knowledge of your Existence in the guise of those things. To experience the state of identity, the utter non-differentiation, you have only to know your Self.

That is again the Spirit-sky (space) in which the mind-sky (space) does appear. That shines within the Heart which is of every thought quite free You are not a thought. You can never be what you think. Inquire and know yourself as innately free of thought. That which shines as the Heart is the Self.

And with gaze fixed within remains fixed as That.
Make your focus steadily nonobjective. If you do so, you remain
as That, without the superimposition of various erroneous no-
tions, from "I" to the forms of the world.

Annamalai (Arunachala), the self-effulgent, shines.
Make your vision nonobjective. Inquire, and the identity abides
as just That. The Absolute shines by itself, to itself. No other is
involved. **but Grace is needed most.** He does not say that
Grace is missing. Grace is needed most, yet Grace is already
there. The ego is needed least; it should be abandoned at once.

so, faithful be unto the Self. Give yourself to That; have
deep conviction in That; listen to That; reflect on That; deeply
meditate on That; worship That in your heart. The result is
Bliss.

II
August, 2011

Om Namo Bhagavate Sri Ramanaya.

Being. Being is the Truth, the Reality that is one without anything else whatsoever. Being is the truth of you, what you really are. It is invariable, entirely bodiless, always real and ever existent, not changing when the body changes, unmoving when the body moves, birthless, and indestructible.

In Being, there is no such thing as other. For Being, there is no such thing as other. Being, without beginning, without end, is. This is the truth regarding you. Unperceived, yet it alone is perceived. Forever unconceived, yet that alone is thought about. Not to be defined in any manner whatsoever, just Being is what is true.

Absorption in Being, in which there is no alternative identity, is the natural state. Let absorption in Being remain as your aim and focus. If you learn to be absorbed in Being, you will have learned everything you need to know in order to be happy and always at peace. Absorption in Being means the cessation of conjuring of imagined definitions—the superimposition of what is not the Self upon the Self. Such absorption is no mere activity of the mind, certainly not an activity of the senses, and, indeed, not an action at all. Absorption in Being, as Being, which is remaining free of any misidentification, constitutes the means for Self-Knowledge. You are Being. Remain absorbed in and as That. Abide as That. Who is there who could do otherwise?

Sri Bhagavan is Being and Being alone. One who knows himself as the Self is only the Self. He can appear to us as if endowed with wondrous attributes, full of grace, compassion, and supremely wise, but the very truth of him transcends every concept of attributes. It is the essence of all these and more, yet there is not the least trace of individuality in him. He is Being, and Being alone. In the motion toward him, which is devotion, one falls, as it were, into his Being, which is absolute, invariable, one without a second, and without an alternative. In the attempt to know him, we must know our own Self, our very Being. In that, all differences vanish.

The best way to listen to and comprehend his teaching is in and from the truth of Being. Here, the meaning of all of it becomes self-evident. The next best way to listen, attempt to comprehend, and thus be absorbed is to have as one's goal the absorption of one's identity in this reality of Being, inquiring into the very nature of the existence of the apparently individualized being, which is regarded as "I." If, in your mind, there is the impression that you are individualized, so that you are in quest of your being, with the "your" part being distinguished from Being, inquire. Inquire into this "my being." The "my"-ness, the "I"-ness, will vanish, or be absorbed, and your identity will remain firmly established in Being, as Being.

What do you assume yourself to be? What truly is your Being? Do you think of yourself as this thing or that thing? Are you dreaming of a body as if it were you or as if it confined you? Who thinks? Who dreams? What is your real nature? Is there the imagination of being an experiencer with form, as someone who wakes, who dreams, who sleeps, as someone who experiences something? For whom is any of that? What is your real Being?

When the Maharshi realized the Self, what was realized? In that realization, there is no possibility of even a trace of difference and no distinction whatsoever between the realizer and the realized. What he realized, what he is, invariably exists, eternally. You ought to realize the same. It is wondrous, indeed, the highest of the high. His spiritual instruction and grace make it perfectly possible. Question deeply, "Who am I?" and abide absorbed as That, Being, itself.

> **Self-Knowledge is an easy thing,**
> **The easiest thing there is.**
> **The Self is something that is entirely real**
> **Even for the most ordinary man;**
> **It could be said that a clear gooseberry**
> **Is an illusion by comparison.**

The analogy pertains to something being entirely self-evident, unmistakable, and that could not be missed.

Self-Knowledge is an easy thing, the easiest thing that **there is.** Self-Knowledge is regarded by all as the supreme attainment, yet he says it is the easiest thing there is. Why? Implicit in the verse is the identification, or equating, of Self-realization with the existence of the Self. If Self-realization were an event, some occurrence, some new attainment, or anything similar, he would not have said that it is the easiest thing there is. What effort is applied to exist? Do you do anything in order to exist?

For the appearance of the mind, much is involved. For the appearance of the senses, the body, and the entire world, much is involved. For your very Being, your very Existence, though, do you do anything in order to make it or to maintain it? It just is. For Self-Knowledge to be declared to be the easiest thing there is, entirely effortless, it must mean that Self-Knowledge is identical with Being.

Then, there is no alternative but to equate Knowledge and Being. If Knowledge is equated with Being, so that it can be the easiest thing there is, it must transcend all thought-forms, all patterns of thinking, all mental modes, conditions, and states.

The Self is something that is entirely real. It is not less real at one time, and more real at another time. What is real always is, and that fully so. We would not say that existence exists less at some time and exists more at another time. Such would be absurd. Existence is invariable and has no alternative. Ideas of existence and nonexistence are not to be equated with Existence itself. Existence, or Being, transcends all of them.

If what is real is that which exists, and therefore the unreal does not exist at all, what does **the Self is something that is entirely real** signify? If the Self is bodiless and, therefore, also boundary-less and indivisible, and if it is entirely real, where is the scope for another, such as the embodied individual? If the Self is entirely real, as it ought to be realized to be, there is no possibility of anyone else or of anything else, of an ego, a world, or any such thing. The Self is the Reality.

That the Self exists, that Being is, is self-evident to everyone, **even for the most ordinary man.** What could possibly be more obvious than your Existence? Even if you suppose, through the delusion that is made of imagination, that you experience something else, and even if you consider it as existent, do you not assume your own existence always? You must exist in order to conceive or perceive anything. You exist without such perception or conception, as well. That you are is so utterly self-evident, never for a moment do you doubt it. Indeed, it is not possible to entertain a doubt about Existence without you existing.

This Existence, without form, without name, undefined, is the real Being. That is truly the Self. It is this Self, the only real Self that there is, that is so self-evident, so obvious, and known by all. Who are all? Just this Existence. So, Self-Knowledge is the easiest thing that there is, for it is Being knowing itself. If you suppose otherwise and think, "It is easy for Sri Bhagavan to say that. He does not realize how difficult it can be," (laughter), what do you regard as yourself? The only apparent difficulty lies in those assumptions. They are, after all, just assumptions and not the truth. The assumptions are difficult, not the Knowledge. To remove such false assumptions by the light of Knowledge is not difficult at all. **Self-Knowledge is the easiest thing** that **there is.** What do you do to know yourself? It is not a doing at all. Who is it that knows the Self? Since there are not two selves, how could there be any difficulty? So, he declares that Self-Knowledge is the easiest thing that there is.

In spiritual practice, all effort is applied toward the negation of misidentification. It is keeping off and destroying erroneous suppositions. For the Knowledge, itself, in which Being shines for itself, there is neither effort nor obstacle. Truly, Self-Knowledge, being devoid of individuality or ego, conforms to no idea, not even to that of "easy." The Knowledge is identical with Being. Being is the Knowledge. Is it easy to exist? Is it hard to exist? Or do you not just exist? Consider deeply how self-evident your Existence is. Nothing else is so. To know, or experience, anything else requires some motion in the mind, but not so your very Being.

Moreover, it is Self-Knowledge, so there is no distinction between that which is known, Being, and that which knows. The

Self is formless, yet entirely real and thus completely self-evident. An objectified notion, however subtle, is not self-evident. It requires imagination, starting with the basic premise, entirely imaginary, of "I."

Existence is entirely real. There is no time when it diminishes. There is no time when it changes. Changefulness is characteristic of the unreal, and what is unreal simply does not exist. One can only loosely think of the unreal as coming and going. It does not actually come at all. If you accept that the Self is real but still think something else comes and goes, you have yet to plunge deeper into what is meant by "entirely real." If something else is believed to be real, as well, the Self is only partially real, or one thing real among many real things. If, though, the Self is entirely real, it is completely the Reality; where is the scope for anything coming and going, and for whom would it come and go?

The Self is something that is entirely real even for the most ordinary man. The nature of the man can be only the same Self. What could possibly be more obvious than your own Being? It is obvious to itself. As there are not two of you, there is no one else to become confused about this. To know how this is true, inquire deeply within, "Who am I"?

> **The Self, which shines as the Sun within the Heart,**
> **Is real and all-pervading. It will reveal**
> **Itself as soon as false thought is destroyed**
> **And not one speck remains. For this thought is**
> **The cause of the appearance of false forms,**
> **The body and the world, which seem to be**
> **Real things in spite of the Self, which steadfast**
> **stands,**
> **The ever-changeless, firm as Truth itself.**
> **When the Self shines forth, darkness will be**
> **dispersed,**
> **Affliction cease, and Bliss alone remain.**

The Self, which shines as the sun within the Heart, is real and all-pervading. Being shines. It is not with a physical light or a subtle light, but it is luminous in the sense of shin-

33

ing as pure Consciousness, referred to as the Sun in the verse. Self-luminous Consciousness is the nature of Being. This Consciousness is real and all pervading, while residing within the heart. What is the heart? It is the very quintessence of your Existence, the very core to which there is nothing interior. At the very core of you, what you truly are, is Being-Consciousness-Bliss. You cannot separate Being from Consciousness. They are one and the same. That which always knows, or shines, is that which exists, and that, indeed, is the Self. That, in truth, you are.

Is real and all-pervading. Is there anywhere in your experience where existence is not? Such would be absurd. Likewise, there is nowhere in your experience where consciousness is not. Just as Being should not be mistaken for a bodily form, so Consciousness should not be mistaken for thought. What lies at the center of you is this Being-Consciousness, the real Self. It is that which actually is, and it is all-pervading. Turn within and discern how this shining Consciousness pervades the entirety of whatever is experienced at any time. So much so is this the case that nothing can be separated as if it existed apart from Consciousness. The forms are entirely pervaded by the Self, to such an extent that it cannot be said that there is an existing "pervaded." Even the imagination does not exist apart from the Existence, or apart from the Consciousness.

The very nature of the subject, the "I," alone is real, and it pervades everywhere. What is at the very center of you is not a small thing. That which is your essence, your heart, is universal. Inquiring "Who am I?" you are not searching for a small thing but, rather, that which is vaster than the vastest.

The Self, which shines as the Sun within the Heart, is real and all pervading. If the Self is actually real, where is the scope for illusion? If it is the sun that shines within the heart of the nature of self-luminous Consciousness, which is the very substance of true Knowledge, and it is all pervading, where is the room for ignorance? Why is it seemingly not realized as such, as non-dual, as One without any alternative? Sri Bhagavan explains, **It will reveal itself as soon as false thought is destroyed and not one speck remains.** Which of your thoughts are false? Which of your thoughts do you regard as false? Which of your thoughts do you regard as valid or true? Those are the ones that still seem to be a veil covering you.

One experiences the Self always whether he knows it or not. To know the Self as it truly is means to know that That alone exists, and That alone is real. While inquiring, the light seems to grow brighter as various false ideas that constitute ignorance are abandoned. The knowledge that the Self alone exists, without there being anything else whatsoever, is the Self directly realized as it is and is revealed when not one speck remains. **Not one speck remains** means none of the content, the delusion of those thoughts, none of the thoughts, and not a trace of the thinker.

The Self will reveal itself when **not one speck remains.** It reveals itself, for there is no second knower. Knowledge belongs entirely to the Self. Ignorance vanishes, and the one who is apparently ignorant vanishes, because such are entirely unreal. You start by eliminating false ideas that delusively give the sense of bondage. When false ideas previously attributed to you are no longer so, they are said to drop off.

How about the one who thinks them? If his nature is questioned, all the particular thoughts about him that form the various vasanas, or tendencies, are destroyed. Then, the very idea that thought exists is brought into question. As long as the content is mistaken to be valid, there is little possibility of actually, decisively discerning that thought, itself, is nonexistent. If the misidentification with the content of thought has already been abandoned, the idea that thought exists comes into question because it depends on the Consciousness imagined as a thinker for whom there are thoughts. If that one is brought into question, all that remains is the self-revelation of Being-Consciousness.

Which of your thoughts do you think are true? If you really knew the false thought as mere false thought, just imagination, it would no longer arise, and there would be no bondage. **It will reveal itself,** the Self will reveal itself, **as soon as false thought is destroyed and not one speck remains.** How do you destroy thought? It is by seeing its falseness. What apparently gives solidity to thought? It is your belief in it. It is the be-

35

lief that it is there and the belief that it is valid. To withdraw that belief and place it in its proper place, in the Reality of the Self, destroys all the thought. Whether they appear to come quickly or slowly, the thoughts do not stand on their own. They have no power of their own. All of the apparent existence, power, and such comes from you. When thought is regarded as playing before you, in relation to the thoughts, you are the witness. When there are no thoughts, such as in deep dreamless sleep, what becomes of the witness? He is not a witness.

That there is existence is indubitable. True Knowledge is utterly thought-transcendent. When thought is destroyed and not one speck remains of the content of your thought, of the idea that there are thoughts, of the thinker who seems to be the individualized knower of thoughts, the Self will reveal itself. This self-revelation is true Knowledge, or the Knowledge of Reality that comprehends Reality as it is.

Otherwise, one can create all kinds of perspectives, such as the Absolute Self plus thought, the Absolute Self plus objects, the Absolute Self plus passivity and dynamism, and the Absolute Self plus power. What about the Self, or the Reality, just as it is? Such is true Knowledge. The rest are, at best, ideas pointing in the right direction. If you pursue single-pointedly an approach that destroys the supposition of "me," making your vision nonobjective, you will understand Reality just as it is.

For this thought is the cause of the appearance of false forms, the body and the world, which seem to be real things in spite of the Self, which steadfast stands, the ever changeless, firm as Truth itself. Thought is the cause of the appearance of false forms. The effect, the form, is nothing but the cause appearing as the effect. Forms, be they gross forms or subtle forms, have no existence, and you have no experience of them, apart from the thought of them. Here, Sri Bhagavan questions the very existence of the world and of the body through which one knows about the world. In a state of mind with thought, you can experience a body and a world, which are the false forms. If there is no thought, there is no body and no world, as in the state of deep dreamless sleep.

Thus, the forms have no existence apart from the thought of them.

The world, the body, and all other objects are composed of thought. Thought always has an objective portion to it. There is no such thing as a nonobjective thought.

Consciousness does not actually become a thought, so objects, therefore, are not actually created. All the forms, the mere appearances, are only thought. Thought is false. When not one speck is seen to actually exist at all, not even so much as the idea of "I," the Self stands in its own light, self-revealed, without any object and without any conception. He indeed expresses the inexpressible. That is called grace.

Thought appears as a body, which is mistaken as a location for the "I," or ego, and, correlating to the body, there is a world. The world is then considered to be the reality, and embodiment is considered to be for the Self. That is illusion; that is the false appearance. The truth is that the world is not real, and you are not the body. The truth is that there is no "this" but "I," and there is no "I" but the one Self.

Being told that duality is unreal, one asks, "How did the duality come to be?" Do you see the silliness of it?

If the world is believed to be real, if you think that you are contained within a body, if you are identified with the body, or if you assume that you are the possessor of a body, there is a need for deeper inquiry, because those are just false appearances, which seem to occur only after thought is mistaken to be real, and the thoughts arise only after the "I."

For this thought is the cause of the appearance of false forms. The very things that seem to veil the nature of Reality are the false forms. They are the body and the world, which seem to be real things. They seem as if real, but from where does the solidity, or reality, come? It does not come from the forms themselves. The world appears, disappears, and reappears, according to the state of mind. From where does the sense of reality, which is constant, come? A body appears, disappears, and reappears, birth after birth. From where does the sense of identity derive? Trace the sense of existence inward to its nature, and thus stand free of all the false form, the false thought.

They **seem to be real things in spite of the Self, which steadfast stands, the ever-changeless, firm as Truth itself.** The world appears and disappears, yet the Self remains. The body appears and disappears, yet the Self remains. It is steadfast. It is not shaken. It remains unchanged always.

The infinite can be known only by means that are infinite. The Knowledge belongs to the Self. The Self cannot be known through the senses or the mind. The Self cannot be known by an ego, which, after all, is an inert illusion. The Self can be known only with its own light, to itself. It is ever-changeless and firm. The world appears and disappears in your experience as you change states of mind—waking, dreaming, and deep sleep--but your Existence does not change. Consciousness does not change. Thought comes, and thought vanishes. The body comes, and the body vanishes. When you think of something, such as the body, the world, etc., it seems as if real. When you do not think of it, there is no question about it.

The Self is not like that though. It is invariable. It does not change but is **firm,** and exists **as truth,** as reality, itself. You are not a thought. You are not a false thought. You are not a thought with borrowed reality, so that it seems as if real. You, the Self, are only the Reality, the Truth itself. Find this Self by tracing within, in a nonobjective manner, that which is changeless. Your body, which is only the imagination or dream of it, is obviously not changeless. Do you have a thought that is changeless, ever-present, and unmoving? All of your thoughts change. The content of your thoughts change, thought appears and disappears, and, when its nature is sought, it is found to be unreal. What is changeless?

The unchanging alone is real. What is changeful cannot be the Truth. If there was a time when something was not, a time when it appears, and a time when it ceases to exist, that something does not truly exist in the middle when it appears. If something is real, it is real always. So, what is always so about you? It cannot possibly be dependent on thought. What this is is utterly unthinkable, yet realized clearly and with certainty, a certainty unknown by thought, the moment the false is abandoned.

When the Self shines forth, darkness will be dispersed. The darkness is ignorance. Does darkness have any substance to it? Can you grab a piece of darkness? Can you slice it or box it? There is no substance to the darkness. Just so is it with illusion, or ignorance. There is no actual substance to it. It is just the appearance of false thought, the thought itself being false, or unreal. So, it is an unreal conception of unreality.

What is Knowledge and whose is it? When false appearance is set aside, or destroyed, Knowledge remains. When the Self shines forth, the Knowledge is for the Self. No individual knows the Self; the Self knows the Self. When you abandon the supposition of being the individual, the thinker of all the false thought, Knowledge shines.

The Self is Knowledge; so, Knowledge knows. That is, the light of Consciousness shines upon itself, yet not as an object. What is the result of such? The ignorance vanishes, **afflictions cease,** and bliss alone remains. All of one's sufferings, in life and in death, are due only to false thoughts that constitute delusion. Without those false thoughts, free of the delusion constituted of misidentification, suffering does not exist. All of one's suffering, without exception, is only illusion born of ignorance. Do away with the ignorance, and affliction ceases. To do away with ignorance, examine its validity. You will find its apparent strength lies in the conceiver of it. Find out the nature of that one, and you are free.

Bliss alone remain[s]. Being-Consciousness-Bliss is a three-fold term for one thing. Just as Being and Consciousness cannot be divided, for they are one and the same, so it is with Bliss. Being is Bliss. Consciousness is Bliss. Create and become caught in false thought, the illusions born of misidentification, and bliss seems to be missing, though it is there all of the time, just as the real Self, or pure Being, seems to be missing, even though it is the only reality the entire time, and Consciousness, which ever knows, seems to be blind or hidden from view. Inquire, so that Consciousness is free of the illusion of thought. Inquire, so that Being is not misidentified with an ego or with a body. In this Knowledge of your Being, of Consciousness as it is, Bliss alone remains. Being alone remains. Consciousness alone remains. Bliss alone remains.

You do not cease to exist. The thinker is a definition that comes and goes. Then, it cannot be a real definition. If something were a real definition of you, it would always be there, just as you are always there. What are you if you are not a thinker? In deep sleep, you experience it. While there is nothing of such a state recorded in your memory, you do know it was very peaceful. Nothing was wrong. The one who existed in deep sleep, with the thinker definition absent, and with all his thoughts absent, is the same one who exists now. Your existence has not changed. Only false ideas, false definitions, have been added, held up only by the strength of this very same unchanging existence.

You are always seeking Reality. For whom does this occur? You say that you keep thinking of the individual. Who is the "I" in that statement? If you inquire deeply into his nature, the rest of your questions are pulled out by the root. Continue to inquire into the nature of your actual Being, your very Existence, and question the purported connection between what you are and what you merely think of, including the body and the world. What you are is untouched by a world, by a body, and by the mind. The untouched one is actually here. Another is just an illusion.

When Consciousness is imagined to be in the form of thought, false appearances, such as the body and the world, appear. If you inquire to know yourself, the very root of illusion is destroyed, and, with it, vanish all of its subsequent creations. By such Knowledge, suffering becomes impossible, and the innate Bliss of your own Being shines for itself. Such everlasting direct experience of your true nature alone constitutes true Knowledge.

The thought "I am the body" is the string
On which are threaded diverse thoughts like beads.
Therefore, on diving deep upon the quest
"Who am I and from where (whence)?"
thoughts disappear,
And Consciousness of the Self then flashes forth

As the "I-I" within the cavity
Of every seeker's Heart, and this is Heaven,
This is that Stillness, the abode of Bliss.

The thought "I am the body" is the string on which are threaded diverse thoughts like beads. Upon this one misidentification, or false conception, that equates the Self with the body, and defines the Self by the attributes of the body, are based innumerable forms of other delusions. The idea that you are in the world is based on the I-am-the-body notion. The very idea that things appear to you is based on the I-am-the-body notion. Examine the workings of your mind. How many ideas are assumed from, and based upon, the position of "I," and, when a form is given to the "I," "I am the body?" Every idea connected with the world is based upon it. Every idea of action and inaction is based upon it. Every idea concerning life and death is based upon it. The regarding of sensations as determining reality is based on the I-am-the-body misconception. Is it true? Are you the body? Did your existence begin with the birth of the body? Will your existence cease with the death of the body? Is your existence limited to a particular shape of so much volume, and of such a size, and of such a mass? Obviously, as a body, you cannot be all-pervading. So, which are you: the body or the infinite, eternal Self?

Therefore, on diving deep upon the quest "Who am I and from where?" Undoubtedly, there is the sense of "I," but what is it? Is it the body? Or is it pure Existence? If, through delusion, you tie the two together, as "I am the body," such is ignorance. Trace the sense of "I." From where does it come? Even to misidentify as "I am the body," there is some power that is identifying. Just as one would trace the reality to arrive at pure Being, likewise trace your sense of identity. From where does "I" come? It does not come from the body. The body does not identify itself as "I." In delusion, one identifies oneself with the body. Trace the power of identifying to its source. Tracing the "I" to its source, inquiring "Who am I?" all of the false assumptions are blown away. What remains?

Thoughts disappear. Every thought based on misidentification disappears, leaving pure Consciousness as the residuum. When such misidentification vanishes by the illuminative power of this inquiry, the **Consciousness of the Self then flashes forth.** Consciousness, as Knowledge, flashes forth, from itself, to itself. No second entity is involved, neither a mind nor an ego—certainly, not the body. The Knowledge of the Self flashes forth to itself, by itself. The inquiry "Who am I?" or "From where does the sense of 'I' come?" destroys the illusion, which is unreal. It does not create a new self for you. There is simply the revelation of the Self as it truly is, no longer mistaken as "I", "I am the body" and all of the other ideas based on such.

The **Consciousness of the Self then flashes forth as the "I-I" within the cavity of every seeker's Heart.** By **cavity** is meant space. The heart of every seeker is the same. It is one Being. There are not different kinds of Being. Everyone includes you. In your heart, in your innermost Existence, will shine the Knowledge indicated by "I-I," as "I am I," the Knowledge of one's true identity, one's actual Existence. When does this shine forth? As soon as the misidentifications associated with the ego and the body are vanquished. When do those disappear? As soon as you actually inquire "Who am I?" and trace your sense of identity to its very source.

This is Heaven, this is that Stillness, the abode of Bliss. Being does not move. The true Self does not ever change. To identify yourself as That alone is at last to be still, and such stillness is heavenly peace. In this peace, there is not the least bit lacking. In the Knowledge of yourself is found the perfectly full Bliss. All this is within you. Just relinquish the tendency to misidentify with the body, by discerning how that cannot possibly be true, and the blissful truth of the Self will shine. It will shine in you, as you.

> **What is the use of knowing everything**
> **Except the Self? What else is there to know**
> **For anyone when the Self, itself, is known?**
> **On realizing in oneself the Self,**
> **Which is the only self-effulgent One**

**In myriads of selves, the Light of the Self
Will clearly shine within. This is, indeed,
The true display of Grace, the ego's death,
And the unfolding of the Bliss supreme.**

Without knowing your own Self, what do you actually know? You merely have thoughts about things, which are only other thoughts. That is not Knowledge. If you want to know what is, you must first know yourself. If not, your idea of what is—be it in a worldly sense or a spiritual sense—is colored by the definition of yourself. The definition of yourself goes into the very makeup of whatever you conceive. First, then, you must know yourself. If you know yourself, your own Being, you find Bliss. If you know anything else but not yourself, how will you be happy?

Without Self-Knowledge, one is only dreaming. If, within a dream, you dream some other dreams about other dream things, it is just dreams upon dreams upon dreams. If you turn inward to know yourself, **what else is there to know for anyone when the Self, itself, is known?** That alone exists. To know anything else without knowing yourself is only illusion. If you turn inward to know yourself, that proves to be the solitary Existence, and there is nothing else.

When, in the common, worldly sense, you know a thing, what actually occurs is that you have a thought about it. That thought about it might be modified over time or prove to be false, and another thought will appear, but it is the thought about it that is provisionally called "knowledge." Self-Realization is contrariwise. When you no longer have a thought about it, it is known. It is precisely in abandoning false conception that one comes to the Knowledge of himself, and the one who so comes to the Knowledge of himself is himself the Knowledge.

If there is "I," there is something else. Where the "I" subsides into real Being, there is no question of anything else. If you are the individual, there is something else to be conceived. Individuality vanishing upon knowing oneself, who is to know what? The Self is one without a second, so there is nothing else to know, and the Self is nonobjective, so there is nothing to be known.

Existence is not an object, though every object is only the Existence. Though your existence cannot be experienced as an object, even as all objects, you experience yourself only. Existence plus the I-am-the-body misconception result in the apparent world of objects. Still, the existence is only one; there is nothing else but that. Abandoning the misidentification, the world vanishes. What remains is pure Existence, which is unmixed, undivided Consciousness.

What is the use of knowing everything except the Self? Can such so-called knowledge bring you happiness? Happiness lies in your Being. Knowledge of your very Being alone is bliss. **What else is there to know for anyone when the Self, itself, is known?** Free of a subject, there is no object for it. The highest Knowledge is attained, and there remains no separate existence apart from the Existence to be known.

On realizing in oneself the Self, which is the only self-effulgent One in myriads of selves, the Light of the Self will clearly shine within. If you dive within to realize what you are, you find that there is only one Self. It is only based on the idea of individuality, with the adjunct of the misconception regarding the body, that one can think of multiple selves. If you are not the body, where is the distinction of so-called "selves"? Interiorly, if the mind is not real, if you are not a thought or a collection of thoughts, where is the distinction of selves such as a "higher self" and a "lower self"? One Self shines as the consciousness of all. If you regard your consciousness as connected with thought and with the body, there seem to be separate selves. That is not actually the case. Divest yourself of the tendency to misidentify with the body or with thought and then say what constitutes multiplicity.

One Self exists, self-luminous and undivided. The one Self is truly you. You ought not to regard anything else as being yourself. The one who shines here and the one who shines there are one Self. They are not two selves of different kinds or two selves of the same kind, but one Self.

This is, indeed, the true display of Grace. Self-revelation is grace. Where there is only one Self, ever luminous and ever free, that is grace. When there is steady abidance in the Knowledge of the one Self which leaves nothing else to be known, that is grace. The Truth shining in your heart so that it will not be covered again is grace. As there is only one Self in myriad selves and actually no multiplicity of selves whatsoever, we cannot really speak of an act of bestowing or receiving grace. What has been said about the self-existent Being and the self-luminous Knowledge, or Consciousness, is true regarding grace as well, and Sri Bhagavan equates the very same with the ego's death and the unfolding of the bliss supreme.

Being is bliss. Imagine Being to be individualized, an ego entity, and bliss seems as if divided or separate from you. What is the truth regarding your nature? What is your Being? If you find your Being, you find Bliss. If you find your Being, you find that you are not limited, for the ego is not real. If you find this unlimited Being, you find unlimited Bliss. What is the ego's death? It is the discovery that it does not exist.

> In order that the bonds of destiny
> And all its kindred may at last be loosed
> And so that one may also be released
> From the dread cycle of both birth and death,
> This path than others is far easier.
> Therefore, be still and keep a silent hold
> On tongue and mind and body. That which is
> The self-effulgent will arise within.
> This is the Supreme Experience. Fear will cease.
> This is the boundless sea of perfect Bliss.

If we are bodies, we are subject to birth and death, karma and destiny, and such. Are we bodies? Inquiring to know our nature is a far easier path because it is direct and does not take for granted the very forms of bondage one is trying to transcend.

Be still and keep a silent hold on tongue and mind and body. Do you know that which is within you that is still, that does not move when the body moves, that does not move when the mind moves, and that does not move even to the extent of going in and out of the Self? What is it that is truly still? This should be realized conclusively.

45

Keep a silent hold on tongue and mind and body. The meaning has relation to the stillness. What is this silent hold to which he refers? How would you hold the body silent? Such an interpretation would make no sense. As long as the body is alive, it makes some noise. If you cannot hear it, someone with a stethoscope can. So, to what is he referring? What is a silent hold on the tongue? It cannot possibly allude to just not speaking, or communicating, for, if that were so, this would not have been said or written. Likewise is it with the mind. Transient mental quietude cannot be that to which he alludes. A silent hold in stillness means not, through imagination, moving out of your true Self and, therefore, not misidentifying with the instruments of the body, speech, and mind. Not to misidentify, not to connect the Self with what is not the Self, precludes the rise of an ego. That in which the ego does not rise is silence. Where no ego notion rises, causing misidentification with the body, speech, and mind, there is the silent hold of the body, speech and mind.

That which is the self-effulgent will arise within. Remove misidentification, and the self-luminous shines.

This is the Supreme Experience. Fear will cease. This is the boundless sea of perfect Bliss. In all of your experience, you hope to find one thing. This one thing is, in truth, yourself. Always, you search for bliss, and bliss is the Self. You always search for yourself. The supreme Knowledge is the supreme experience. If you know That, you know what needs to be known. If you experience That, you experience what needs to be experienced. If you know That is yourself, you truly have Knowledge.

Fear will cease. Where there is duality, as it were, there is fear. The root of duality is the ego, or "I-notion." Fear is the idea, the assumption, that existence will cease to exist and, since one intuits that his existence is his happiness, that his happiness will cease to exist. When we think that existence-bliss will cease to exist and cease to be blissful, there is fear. When there is another, there can be fear of another. When we inquire and know the Self as it is—the only one, the self-luminous one, the all-pervading Reality—there is no "another." There is no cessation of

Existence, and there is no destruction of our Bliss. How will one who, by inquiring, has realized this conclusively experience fear?

The birth of the ego is the beginning of fear. The death of the ego is the end of fear. The death of the ego happens for anyone who inquires "Who am I?"

Blissful Being is your real nature. The ego is but an ignorant notion. Your Existence shall never cease to exist, and your Existence is all the bliss you could ever need. In order to give rise to fear or other forms of suffering, you must first conceive of yourself as distinct from this blissful Existence—the vast, formless, real Self; you must first think of yourself as an individual. Then, what the individual has or loses, such as a body, becomes the expression of his fear or suffering. To become fearless, Sri Ramana recommends the easier path, "Who am I?"

> **Annamalai, the Transcendental One,**
> **That is the Eye behind the eye of the mind,**
> **Which eye and other senses cognize[s],**
> **Which, in their turn, illuminate the sky (space),**
> **And all the other elements, as well.**
> **That is, again, the Spirit-sky (space) in which**
> **The mind-sky (space) does appear;**
> > **That shines within**
> **The Heart which is of every thought quite free,**
> **And, with gaze fixed within, remains as That.**
> **Annamalai, the self-effulgent, shines.**
> **But Grace is needed most. So, faithful be**
> **Unto the Self, and Bliss will then result.**

Annamalai is a name for Arunachala, and, in a footnote, the translator gives the meaning as "insurmountable hill." Of course, people do climb to the top of it, so its insurmountableness must be of a different nature.

All of the elements of matter are perceived by the senses. All of the senses are perceived by the mind. Something perceives the mind. That is transcendent of the elements, the senses, and the mind. That is the infinite Consciousness. No one can surmount that, but you can be absorbed into it. Absorption is for the one who is of **every thought,** every false notion, **quite free.**

47

With gaze fixed within remains as That. To turn inward to know yourself and cease to misidentify with what is objective is the **gaze** referred to. It is to remain as That, as the Self, and to no longer mistake yourself to be something else, apparently moving out of yourself, which is absurd. If your gaze is thus fixed within so that you remain as That, not as a mind, not as the senses, not as a body or anything of a material nature, but your identity remains just as That, this is Self-Realization. **The self-effulgent shines.** The Reality comprehends itself, and you, yourself, are the Reality.

Grace is needed most. So, faithful be unto the Self, and Bliss will then result. Be true to yourself. If you want happiness that does not depend on a cause, has no condition, and never comes to an end—as all living beings naturally desire—you must know yourself. Grace is needed most, but grace is not different than the Self. The Self is self-luminous. The Knowledge is already there. Through inquiry put an end to the misidentification; that is being faithful to yourself. If that much is accomplished, all is complete.

III

August, 2012

Om Namo Bhagavate Sri Ramanaya

Unmoving abidance in the unmoving, as the unmoving, is the significance of Sri Bhagavan's arrival at Arunachala. What is it to be unmoving? The least deviation from the absolute, perfect Reality, even so much as the thought of "I," is not there. He abides in himself, as himself, for, between the absolute Self and Sri Bhagavan, there is not the least bit of differentiation. This unmoving state, this unmoving Being, is the root of his illimitable grace and his boundless wisdom.

To abide by his teachings, and to become keenly aware of his grace, is similarly to dwell in the unmoving. This to such an extent that there is no one who dwells in the unmoving, but rather one dwells in the unmoving as the unmoving. What moves? What does not move? One should discriminate.

He arrived at Arunachala, and he stayed there ever after. What does it signify? It signifies Realization of the unmoving One and no illusion of separation or deviation. For us, he became a wondrous sadguru, yet he remains as the unmoving, undifferentiated One. For us, his very name is associated with boundless grace, yet he remains unmoving, without the least notion of false distinction or separation. For us, with his Knowledge, he explains everything, yet he remains as the inexplicably unmoving One.

We, also, by the power of that grace and the illumination of that Knowledge, should arrive at the unmoving One. Once having arrived, never depart. It is the state of Self-Knowledge. It is such a state of knowledge that the Knowledge, itself, is of the nature of our very Being. If it is of the nature of our very Being, once realized, there is no departure from it, just as one does not depart from one's own existence. Siva himself arrived at Siva and remained in Siva as Siva. Siva should be realized as one's true and only Self.

What moves and what does not move? Bodies move, thoughts move, worlds move, and states move. Something does

49

not move. What is that which does not move? To misidentify as the moving and thus think that you move in and out of the unmoving is absurd. By deeply inquiring "Who am I?" let your identity be established as the unmoving, which naturally remains without moving from itself. To think that you go into the Self and that you exit the Self is not right. All the while, there is something unmoving, and that unmoving One alone is your Self.

Sri Bhagavan has made himself known in your heart. Adhering to the teachings he has graciously provided, you will be at peace, entirely free, as the unmoving, with all doubts or differences dissolved forever.

> **Self-Knowledge is an easy thing,**
> **The easiest thing there is.**
> **The Self is something that is entirely real**
> **Even for the most ordinary man;**
> **It could be said that a clear gooseberry**
> **Is an illusion by comparison.**

Self-Knowledge is an easy thing, the easiest thing there is. What is the easiest thing that there is? That which is not an attainment, but is ever-existent, must be recognized as being the easiest thing that there is. If something is not ever-existent, there is some activity required to bring it about. That would not be the easiest thing there is. The easiest thing must be the ever-existent. What is ever-existent? The Self is ever-existent. It is not something to be attained anew, nor is it ever more or less at any time, but it is ever-existent, and that, fully so. So, the Self must be understood to be the easiest thing.

The Realization of the Self, which consists of Self-Knowledge, must necessarily be of the very same nature as the Self itself. Otherwise, there would be the illusion of duality, and such is not the Reality. Similarly, for Self-Knowledge to be the easiest thing there is, such Realization must be of an ever-existent nature.

What always is is the easiest thing that there is. So easy is it, so innate is it, that it is difficult even to describe it in terms of "difficult" and "easy." It transcends all such ideas. The text, though, says **the easiest thing there is.** The Self is ever-existent. It is the easiest thing. Self-Knowledge is natural. It is the easiest thing. The Realization of this Self-Knowledge comes by profound inquiry, which is primarily a negation of the false, so that the real Self stands self-revealed. What could possibly be difficult in negating that which is false? What could be easier than abandoning the unreal as unreal? After all, it has no weight, and it has no substance.

The Self is something that's entirely real. The analogy of the clear gooseberry in one's hand refers to how self-evident it is. What could be more evident than your very existence? Your very existence always exists. It is there when things are perceived and when things are not perceived. It is there when there is thought and when there is no thought. What could possibly be more obvious than the fact of your existence?

What is the nature of this existence? Realization of such is Self-Knowledge. Self-Knowledge is the easiest thing that there is. It is difficult to pretend to be a self that you are not, rather than be the Self that you truly are. It is difficult to conjure up and to maintain ignorance, which is forsaken for being nonsensical if it is so much as questioned. It is difficult to overlook the fundamental existence and take something else to be real. To abide in the Self, as the Self, in complete Knowledge of the Self, is the easiest thing that there is. To comprehend this, do not think in terms of tasks that are difficult or easy. This is supreme ease, of the nature of the ever-existent.

Inwardly inquire to realize the ever-existent within you. What is it that exists always? What exists always for you, without a beginning or an end and without an interruption? Certainly, such is not the body or the mind. They are not forever. They are not continuous. What is the ever-existent? Certainly, it is not a state of mind or a condition of the body or senses. These come and go. Search for that which is ever-existent. That which has the capacity to know it is that. Because, here, there is no distinction, no difference, between the knower and the known, it is the easiest thing that there is. Inquire within, and discern that which is ever-existent. You need not create it anew, so it is the easiest thing that there is, for it already exists. Nothing need be added to it. There is only the need of knowing it as it is.

The Self is something that is entirely real, not partially so, and not only in the past or the future or the present. It is entirely real. If the Self is entirely real, nothing else is so.

Remain with the self-evident Being. The ever-existent is the self-existent. This, indeed, is truly your Being. The abandonment of contrary false concepts, which constitutes the method, is as easy as the self-evident Being. You exist. What do you need to do to make it so? You know that you exist. What do you need to do in order to create this knowledge? Nothing. The nature of this existence, the nature of this knowledge, is the Absolute Brahman.

Nothing is as self-evident as your very Existence. The Self is that which is ever-existent. That which is not ever-existent is not your Self. What exists always, without a break? Identify yourself as that which is ever-existent, and you find the Knowledge of this ever-existent Self to be identical with Being. The Knowledge of your Self is as ever-existent as the Self. Who becomes ignorant? Is that one ever-existent? If he is not so, he is not the Self, and your Self must be otherwise.

Ignorance is a mistake. If the mistake is made, there is someone for whom it occurs. Inquire to know that someone, and the mistake vanishes, because it is not real. In speaking about Self-Knowledge as an easy thing, the emphasis in the verse is more about the absence of activity or of a new attainment and the ever-existent nature of this knowledge, than it is a comment on effort applied in spiritual practice. If the Self is misidentified with the mind, senses, and the body, effort of some kind should be applied to become free. If one knows his nature to be transcendent of activity, subtle as well as gross, beyond the body, the senses, and the mind, the ever-existent nature of that bodiless, mind-transcendent Self becomes the basis for this great ease.

This ever-existent nature is not only true for the great rishis; it is true for everyone. It is the Self of all. Hence, he says **the most ordinary man.**

The Self is something that is entirely real. How real is real? Conversely, how unreal is unreal? Unreal simply is not. Real is that which truly exists. Now and always, the nature of your very existence is the Self, and that entirely so. There is no one else. By inquiry, supported by his grace, realize this conclusively, and illusion appears no more. To establish your identity as That, which is to realize it conclusively, all you need do is deeply, thoroughly inquire, "Who am I?"

Having in the previous verse declared the immediacy and the self-evident nature of the Self, Sri Bhagavan in the next verse says:

> The Self, which shines as the Sun within the Heart,
> Is real and all-pervading. It will reveal
> Itself as soon as false thought is destroyed
> And not one speck remains. For this thought is
> The cause of the appearance of false forms,
> The body and the world, which seem to be
> Real things in spite of the Self, which
>   steadfast stands,
> The ever-changeless, firm as Truth, itself.
> When the Self shines forth, darkness will be
>   dispersed,
> Afflictions cease, and Bliss alone remain.

The Sun within the Heart refers to self-luminous Consciousness, which is identical with the quintessential Being, or pure Existence. **The Self which shines as the Sun within the Heart** is the Existence, which shines as pure Consciousness, and that **is real and all-pervading.**

Of all things known, of what can you be certain? The objective portion is never certain. Indeed, it is not real. Of that which shines as knowing, though, you can be quite sure. This knowing, or Consciousness, pervades all that you ever experience. This pervades all utterly, to the extent that there is no other all or substance involved. The Consciousness is the Existence. It is what is real. It is all-pervasive. Do you ever experience anything apart from the Consciousness that knows? The Consciousness pervades the entirety of the experience, from the smallest to the vastest.

It will reveal itself as soon as false thought is destroyed, and not one speck remains. If Being-Conscious-

53

ness is self-evident, immediate, existing always, and all-pervasive, so that there is no way that you can be apart from it or outside of it, why is it that it seems as if it is not experienced? Why is it not known as it is? Such is due only to false thought. The thought is false in a two-fold manner. What one thinks of is unreal, or false, and the thought, itself, is false and not real.

Not one speck remains includes the thought that there is such a thing as thought. Besides the one Self, which alone exists eternally and shines as the self-luminous Consciousness, what else do you think exists? "I," "this," your supposed self, and something else, are the false thoughts that are to be destroyed. How is every speck of it destroyed? It is destroyed by the knowledge that it is false. It seems to be substantial only so long as you believe it to be true, to be the reality. The unreal vanishes into the nothingness that it is, as soon as you discern that it is unreal. Of the thoughts that you may entertain in your mind, which of any of them are you willing to continue to assume is true or real?

Bondage and illusion are nothing but the thought of such. This thought seems to veil the true nature of Being-Consciousness-Bliss. Destroy such thought, by discerning that it is inapplicable. The Self is free from thought. Not a single thought pertains to it. The Self is the Reality, and not a single thought pertains to the Reality.

The Self is not some small, individualized thing, but it is real and all-pervading. **Entirely real** means that it is one without an alternative. First comprehend that the thought does not pertain to the Reality of the Self. From there, realize that the thought itself does not exist as such. It is false thought and unreal thought. There is nothing substantial to bondage or illusion whatsoever.

By what power do you see the false as false, so that the Reality shines for itself? It is by the power inherent in the self-luminous Consciousness. It manifests as the discriminative inquiry, "Who am I?" that determines non-objectively what, indeed, is the Self and that relinquishes the misidentification with what is not the Self. Existence is always. You are ever-existent. Consciousness is always. Knowledge is ever-existent. Realize this knowledge of your own nature. Discern what in truth you really are. That which so discerns and knows certainly is not the senses and not the mind, which consists of false thought, but something that is innately transcendent of the mind and beyond thought. Thought is not able to discriminate between who you are and thought, but you can, and you are not a thought.

For this thought is the cause of the appearance of false forms, the body and the world, which seem to be real things in spite of the Self, which steadfast stands, the ever-changeless, firm as Truth itself. The appearance of anything objective, which has form, is merely the thought of such. Just as in a dream, the body and world that appear in the dream are merely the thoughts of such and do not exist independently, so it is with the experience in the waking state. All that you know of the world is just your thought of it. The Self is real and all-pervading. Seeing a world where there is, in truth, only the Self is the appearance of false thought. Such is mere delusion and not the truth at all.

The ideas of multiple persons delineated by bodies and multiple minds inhabiting those bodies are entirely just more thought forms. Consciousness remains unformed, unembodied, and not multiple. In a dream, you are rarely alone. There are other dream characters, and, generally, they corroborate your experience. When you wake up, though, are you prepared to say that there were different people there, and that they saw these same things? Of course not. Just this unreal, false thought appears as an individualized, embodied subject, and is capable of appearing as if multiple subjects and multiple objects. Such subject and object Sri Bhagavan has compared to that of a movie, in which is portrayed a king, and, before the king, some drama is enacted. The king is the subject. The drama is the objective part of this experience. Both the king and the drama are not real. They are just images on a screen. The screen, though not seen as an image in the film, is the only thing actually there. So it is with the subject and object of experience. In a dream, for the dream character, there appear to be other dream characters and objects, but what actually is there, pervading the entire dream? The only thing actually present is the Consciousness, which is invisible in the dream. So, what is seen is not there, and what cannot be seen is alone there.

Each state seems more real while it is occurring. Each one seems preposterous and is rejected when it is not occurring. In deep sleep, both dream and waking are gone. You are the Existence-Consciousness-Bliss that continuously exists during all of those three states. They come and go. You do not come and go. You remain unmoving. They depend on you in order to appear. You do not depend upon them. You are the self-existent One. The things, including the activities, events, and experiences, that appear in each state are composed of each state. So the waking state composes the waking state experience, just as the dreaming state composes the dreaming state experience. You, though, in your real nature, are not composed of anything else. You are not a state. You are Existence. Anything that appears within a state of mind you are not. In this present waking state, a body and a world appear. None are you. If you are not the body and not in the world, what are you?

Knowing yourself to be, in reality, pure Consciousness, discern that which is a mere product of thinking—all the false forms, including the body and the world—and know them to be unreal.

This thought is the cause of the appearance of false forms, the body and the world, which seem to be real things, in spite of the Self, which steadfast stands, the ever-changeless, firm as Truth, itself.

The nature of forms is that they are unreal, for the Existence of the Self alone is present. A characteristic of the unreal is that the unreal changes, while the Reality must always be so. That which is truly the Self is always so and never changes. What do you regard as yourself that changes? What is it that does not change? The changeless is the Truth. The changeless alone is actually the Self. Anything that changes just by a change of thought cannot be you. If there is thought of it, the world appears. If there is no thought of it, the world vanishes. If there is thought of it, there is a body. With the absence of thought, where is the body? So it is with all forms. The formless, ever-existent Self, which you truly are, is unchanging. Know yourself to be unchanging and formless, and you abide **as** the **Truth, itself.**

How do the body and the world appear? It is just by your thought of such. How does thought appear as if real? It is your belief in such. The root of such belief, the source of the quality of being real, is your essential Existence, which is of the nature of pure Consciousness. If false thought is abandoned, the reality, is not lent to things that are not real.

The ever-changeless, firm as Truth, itself speaks of your actual Existence and not some other existence. The idea of "other" is just false thought. He speaks of our very Being, the egoless, bodiless Self.

When the Self shines forth, darkness will be dispersed, affliction cease, and Bliss alone remain. Ignorance is compared to darkness. Does darkness have any substance? If, with a lamp, you look for darkness, what do you find? The lamp, here, is your inquiry to know the Self, the light of which is the Knowledge innate to the Self. If you examine the false thoughts that take the form of misidentifications, with the light of inquiry, the misidentifications vanish. The darkness of ignorance disperses. It ceases to exist, because it has no substance to begin with.

If you so inquire, freeing yourself of misidentification with the body, the world, and such, affliction ceases, and bondage becomes impossible. When you are not bound you are free of suffering. He has revealed your nature as Being, as Consciousness, and now as Bliss. Afflictions cease, and bliss alone remains. This Bliss is identical with your Being, and it remains alone, just as Being remains alone. There is no other reality.

Being-Consciousness-Bliss are not three characteristics, but rather a three-fold description of one, ineffable Reality. The Reality is the Self. False thought, erroneous conception, makes it appear as other than you and you other than it. When, in imagination only, you stand as other than it, it seems that there are other differences, as well. Turn within. Examine your mind. Determine which false thoughts you believe, and inquire to know who you really are. If you would treat every thought just as a mere thought and not as anything true, in what way could you be bound? In what way would you suffer? Such would not be possible. Knowing the unreal to be unreal is its end. Knowing a false idea is just a false idea, just imagination, is its end.

Bhagavan says,

The thought "I am the body" is the string
On which are threaded diverse thoughts like beads.
Therefore, on diving deep upon the quest
"Who am I and from where (whence)?" thoughts
    disappear,
And Consciousness of the Self then flashes forth
As the "I-I" within the cavity
Of every seeker's Heart. And this is Heaven,
This is that Stillness, the abode of Bliss.

How many of your ideas are based on the premise of being the body? If the I-am-the-body conception is not true, the basic premise for all these other ideas is not true. The entire samsara has a fundamental flaw: It is the I-am-the-body misconception. See how the I-am-the-body misconception is woven into ever so many ideas.

Ask yourself if you are the body. "I am born, I live, I die," are misidentification with the body. "I change, I act, I do, I stop doing," are misidentification with the body. "I am here, I am there, I am then, I am now," all of this is misidentification with the body. "I am in a world, there are others to whom I relate," all of that is based on misidentification with the body. "I am young, I am old, I am healthy, I am infirm, I come, I go," all that is based on misidentification with the body. "I am tired, I am energetic," are misidentification with the body. None of those characteristics, and ever so many more of the same, are yours, if you liberate yourself from the misconception of being a body.

How could you be a body? It may be a predominant thought, but how could it be true? The body is not **ever-changeless, firm as Truth, itself.** What you seek to realize in your inquiry is that which is entirely bodiless. It has no bodily signs, and it is not a bodily experience. It is abidance utterly free of the I-am-the-body misconception.

One should be **diving deep upon the quest "Who am I and whence?"** "Who am I?" means to determine what your Self actually is, not by thinking, for thought is false, but by Self-Knowledge, which is thought-transcendent, just as knowledge of existing right now and the shining of Consciousness right now are already thought-transcendent. Likewise is the experience of bliss. **Whence** does not mean from within the body, from one position in the body or another. It means to trace where the sense of "I" derives. The focus is your sense of existence, your sense of identity. This does not mean the senses, such as seeing, hearing, touching, etc. It means the interior knowledge of "I," of existing. From where does that derive? It does not come from the body. You are not the body, and your sense of existence does not come from the body. If you comprehend this, you are immortal, and so is your happiness.

On diving deep upon the quest "Who am I and whence?" thoughts disappear, and [the] Consciousness of the Self then flashes forth. Why do the thoughts disappear? They disappear because they are based on the I-am-the-body misconception. If you inquire "Who am I? From where am I? From where does the sense of existence come?" you see that the Self has nothing to do with the body. Your existence is bodiless and does not derive from the body. With your sense of existence disentangled from the form of the body, all of the thoughts that are based on the confusion of thinking "I am this body" dissolve. If every false thought that is based on the misconception that assumes you to be a bodily entity were to vanish, what would remain? The **Consciousness of the Self then flashes forth.** It shines without a veil; it shines for itself, by itself. This is not known by another; it knows itself. It shines, or flashes forth, **as the "I-I" within the cavity of every seeker's Heart.** Within, in the quintessence of your Being, you realize that "I am I, and nothing but I." Thought makes it appear that you are some thing. That fundamental something is the body. Inquiring to know who you are, inquiring to determine where the sense of identity or reality derives, you find that you are not anything that can be conceived. You are only "I." What is "I"? It is not the body. It is ever changeless, so it cannot be the ego, which rises and falls as it is assumed.

If you treat the vastness that is free of thought as if it were some passing experience and the experiencer of such as if individualized, who then goes on, after the experience is over, to experience something else, what is the nature of that experiencer? The Existence cannot be determined as if it were an objective sphere of experience beyond you. Existence must be known as your existence. The very idea that you are an individual, who experiences things high and low and vast and limited, should be examined. That very "I" should be inquired into thoroughly. Is that one a body? Is that one actually individualized? Is that one anything conceived in thought? It is the nature of ignorance to invert, to make the real seem as if unreal and the unreal as if real. It makes the Self appear as not the Self and what is not the Self as the Self. So, even though the body and thoughts are not the Self, they are mistaken to be the definition of the Self. Even though that which is transcendent of thought, of the nature of absolute Being-Consciousness-Bliss, is the Self, it is treated as if it were some object that comes and goes, is lost and needs to be attained. The inversion of ignorance can be easily destroyed by inquiring as to what one really is.

If you can discern that objects are not objects but just thought, that is wonderful. If you question the validity of thought, that is better. If you inquire for whom are these thoughts and, thus, for whom is all the objectified experience, and, by such inquiry, the sense of identity and reality return to their origin, that is best.

The content of thought is an unreal appearance composed only of thought. The thought, itself, is false. It does not exist as such. There is no substance to this illusion. If you have the conviction that sat-chit-ananda is the Reality, but, in your experience, it is not yet fully the case, examine what makes it appear as if it were not the case. What misidentification is in the illusion, so that it appears that that which alone exists, is real, and is all-pervading is not fully so? In truth, it is already fully so. If you think otherwise, it is just dreaming. To wake from the dream, inquire "Who am I? Whence am I?"

The dream of delusion is just thought upon thought. It is based on one false assumption, the first thought. Inquiry directs you there. **The thought "I am the body" is the string on which are threaded** the **diverse thoughts like beads.** If you realize that you are not the body, what happens to delusion's dream? If you continue in this spirit of inquiry, the Consciousness of the Self flashes forth, full of bliss, as your very Existence. **And this is Heaven, this is that Stillness, the abode of Bliss.** It is the perfection of happiness. It is what is meant by "stillness," or "silence," and it is the peace that is indescribable. It is the stillness of the unmoving Reality, which never deviates from itself.

> **What is the use of knowing everything**
> **Except the Self? What else is there to know**
> **For anyone when the Self, itself, is known?**
> **On realizing in oneself the Self,**
> **Which is the only self-effulgent One**
> **In myriads of selves, the Light of the Self**
> **Will clearly shine within. This is, indeed,**
> **The true display of Grace, the ego's death,**
> **And the unfolding of the Bliss supreme.**

What is the use of knowing everything except the Self? Unless you know the Self, the knower of all that is known, what do you really know? Can false thought be regarded truly as knowledge? Unless you know yourself, what do you know? The definitions of oneself go into the very fabric of whatever you think that you perceive.

Unless the Self is known, Reality is not known, for the Self is pure, limitless Existence. If we know something, but do not know the existence of that something, what do we really know? The Self is unalloyed Consciousness, which is the very substance of all knowing, of all knowledge. Unless the Consciousness is known, what is it that one is calling "knowledge"?

The Self is the repository of bliss. What is the use of knowing ever so many things if they do not conduce to your happiness? Knowledge of the Self alone shows what is bliss.

What else is there to know for anyone when the Self, itself, is known? Knowing the Self is the fullness of Bliss. The

Knowledge of the Self is the Knowledge of Reality. It is the finality. If you inquire deeply and know yourself as, in truth, you are, you know all there is to be known. You know that which ought to be known, in this very life.

The idea that there is something else, unknown or to be known, is based upon a supposition regarding oneself. Everything that one thinks one knows, from the smallest to the largest, is based on what view of the subject, the knower? For there to be a "this," there must be an "I." For there to be a world, there must be a body. For there to be a collection of thoughts, there must be a supposed mind. If, in knowing oneself, the tendency to misidentify with the body, the senses, and the mind, or as an ego, is abandoned, one's own infinite, eternal Existence is revealed to itself. What else is there to be known? By whom would it be known? **What else is there to know for anyone when the Self, itself, is known?**

When the Self is not known as it truly is, there seems to be something else to know. What is the use of knowing that something else, which is just a mirror-image of one's misidentification? The misidentification resolved, one knows one's real Being. For that, there is no other-ness and no difference. It is infinite, eternal, and homogeneous, without the least trace of difference. There is nothing inside it or outside it to be known.

All of the known depends on the Consciousness that knows such. When the consciousness is assumed to be individualized, there is something else to be known. Inquire directly into your consciousness and discern its non-individualized, non-particularized, self-luminous nature. While referred to as the knower of all, it is unknown, for it is nonobjective; it is not a knower, but pure Consciousness.

The only substance in the knower is the Consciousness, but it is not individualized. The only substance in the known is the very same Consciousness, but it is not objective. The only substance, the only existence, present in the knowing is the same Consciousness, but it is not a form of relation. If from knowledge the objective portion is negated, as being merely an illusion, Consciousness alone remains, and that is oneself.

Consciousness is transcendent of the mind. The modes of mind are not stable. When it is in a sattvic mode, peacefully and keenly alert, make the best use of it. When it is in the form of another guna, still you should make the best use of it, by recognizing where you are in relation to that, which is not in that at all. You are beyond the mind. The belief that you are in the mind, or traveling through the mind, should be thoroughly questioned.

If you admit the appearance of a mind, it appears in you, but ignorance makes it seem as if you appear in it. You are not in it; it is in you. You are space-like and unaffected. Waking comes, you are. Dreaming comes, you are. Deep sleep comes, you are. Any state may come, you are. Samadhi may come, still you are. In that changeless "you are" is found the Truth and your freedom.

Whether one speaks more or less or the same may vary according to circumstances and temperament, but the wise do not waste time. When you have the precious opportunity to realize what the Maharshi has revealed, the supreme blissful Truth, why waste time? When you can inquire, why waste time thinking of something else? When you can be happy, why waste time being sorrowful?

On realizing in oneself the Self, which is the only self-effulgent One among the myriad of selves, **the Light of the Self will clearly shine within.** The Self is your withinness. To dive within is to abide free of misidentification with what is actually without. Your within-ness is absolute Being, the changeless, consistent, invariable Existence. The nature of this Existence is Consciousness. It is the only self-effulgent one. Everything shines by its light. It draws its light from nowhere else. Consciousness is self-effulgent. Sensations are not so. Mental conceptions of any kind are not so. Look to that in you which is self-knowing, self-luminous.

How is it that you know? Just as you do not do anything in order to be, you do not do anything in order to know. Knowledge is not an activity. Activity cannot yield liberation, but Knowledge is liberation. The self-luminous nature of Consciousness, free of misidentification, is the Realization, itself. It is inherently free of even the least trace of bondage. **The only self-effulgent One in myriads of selves, the Light of the Self will clearly shine within.** There are not multiple selves.

It is not at all true to think of your self and somebody else's self. It is not true to think in terms of the Self and your self, or of a higher self and a lower self. There is only one Self. If you conceive of having a higher self and a lower self, what is the Self of those selves? The Existence is only one and is not so divided. If you think in terms of self and others, is not this just a division of bodies?

Consciousness and the idea of a multiplicity of selves, a multiplicity of minds, is like the sun, which is obviously just one, pouring its light down on platters filled with water that act like a reflecting medium. As many platters of water that are placed there, just so many reflections appear. The sun is only one. The light is only one. Only the limiting adjuncts, the form of the platter, make it seem as if individualized. Similarly, Consciousness is only one. The Self is only one. Only the limitations superimposed upon it in imagination, born of the I-am-the-body misconception, make it appear as if multiple. Associate the Consciousness with the body, and you think of a mind. The mind's supposedly being contained within a body seems to be multiple minds. The nature of the Consciousness, set free of the misconception of being the body, or of being defined by the body, is absolutely one and undivided. So, his consciousness is your consciousness, and there is not another kind of consciousness. Misidentify, through imagination, and conjure up all kinds of false thought, and it seems so different. There is he, there are you, there is the supreme consciousness and your own consciousness, etc. The Reality is not like that at all. When realizing in oneself the Self, not a self, but the Self, which is the only self-effulgent one in myriads of selves, the light of the Self will clearly shine with Knowledge. Recognize your nature as this indivisible Consciousness.

This is, indeed, the true display of Grace, the ego's death, and the unfolding of the Bliss supreme. Grace is shown in innumerable ways. It would not be possible to enumerate them all. The shining forth of the Self, for itself, in itself, to itself, all by itself, is the true display of grace. It is also the ego's death. There is no room in this truth for the notion of a separate individuality. The direct way to bring about the death of the ego and the revelation of such grace is to inquire "Who am I?" As the ego is the source of all that is futile and of the nature of suffering in life, its death, which is the realization of its utter nonexistence, is the **unfolding of the Bliss supreme.** Supreme bliss is the very nature of the Self, the very nature of Being. It seems veiled or limited due only to false thought, the first of which is the ego notion. The veil is burnt up by profound inquiry. The unfiltered happiness of the Self shines freely.

So, knowing the Self is knowing what ought to be known. Abiding as the Self is being as you really exist. The happiness of such leaves nothing else to be desired, ever.

> **In order that the bonds of destiny**
> **And all its kindred may at last be loosed,**
> **And so that one may also be released**
> **From the dread cycle of both birth and death,**
> **This path than others is far easier;**
> **Therefore, be still and keep a silent hold**
> **On tongue and mind and body. That which is**
> **The self-effulgent will arise within.**
> **This is the Supreme Experience. Fear will cease.**
> **This is the boundless sea of perfect Bliss.**

You do not belong in the sea of birth and death—samsara. You do not belong in the state of being an embodied being driven by destiny or karma. Such is not what is natural for you. One suffers in such a state, and one desires to be free. The desire to be free is the call of your own Self to itself to be awake to itself.

To gain such freedom, to be released from such karma, or destiny, to be free from the dreaded cycle of birth and death, the cycle of illusion and suffering, **this path than others is far easier.** What is this path? How would it be possible to abide as the Self except by inquiring and knowing oneself as the Self is? This path is easier because of its directness. This path is easier because what you use is innate, your own Consciousness to know your own Existence. This path is easiest because it is mind-transcendent. This path is easiest because it begins at the end; there is not a long way to travel.

Therefore, be still and keep a silent hold on tongue and mind and body. What is stillness? Stillness is the destruction of all name and form, which is liberation from all that is conceived and perceived. Such is silence. Stillness indicates remaining unmoved from your real nature. Since it is not possible for you to go out of your own Existence, such stillness implies the cessation of imagination, the cessation of misidentification. If you cease to think of yourself as an "I," as a body, and in terms of the qualities of these, you are still. If you identify yourself wholly with the Existence, which is absolutely changeless, the timeless, the location-less, you are still. If you do not give rise to the ego notion, the sense of "I" and "mine," you are still. If you do not imagine a world and entrance into it, you are still.

What is the silent hold? The silence is the same not imagining a deviation from the Self. Absence of the ego is stillness, or silence. A silent hold is to not let the ego arise in relation to the mind, body, or speech. This includes having no ego notion arise in terms of what is done in, or by, the body, what is communicated or related in speech, and what is thought of in the mind. Keep a silent hold. That is, give no scope to the ego notion whatsoever.

It may be a common assumption that to be free from thought means that one cannot think about something. The idea is that one should not think, so one cannot plan; one should be spontaneous to be free and so should not engage in any planning. None of that, though, has anything to do with finding one's real Existence. If you perform action in the spirit of selfless service, that ego-dissolving selfless service shines by the light of Knowledge.

The action may be said to be neutral. It is neither binding nor liberating. If you misidentify as a body and perform action for egotistical purposes, it appears as if binding. If performed selflessly, as worship, for purposes of meditation, etc., it is ego-dissolving, and it is beneficial and liberating. The orientation matters supremely. The orientation has everything to do with your knowledge, or what you regard as your identity.

The comprehension that it is the Self that is loved and served is definitely in keeping with Knowledge of the Truth.

Similarly, an offering is not because of something intrinsic to the action, but because of a deeper knowledge. With this understanding, you have an offering, and the result of that does not decay. If one questions the purpose and one is in earnest, the purpose will be to worship Bhagavan. Of course, who are we to stand apart from him to worship him? So, he is in charge of that, too. Everything becomes him; everything becomes his. If there is doing, he alone does; and he provides the means by which to offer to him.

When engaged in what would otherwise appear to be worldly activity, you can dedicate the ultimate fruits of such activity to a spiritual purpose. It is also most important to realize that you are not the performer of action, because you are not the body. If that is understood and this approach is taken, there will be no bondage due to action.

That which is the self-effulgent, pure Consciousness, will arise within. It will shine freely, unveiled by imagination. **This is the Supreme Experience.** The shining of Consciousness, by itself, to itself, is supreme. It is the only true experience. The rest is just imagination.

Fear will cease. When is there fear? When there is duality, as it were. When is there duality? When the notion "I" arises. If you realize your nature by profound inquiry to be just the self-effulgent Consciousness, the one Self, free of the idea of different selves, fear and duality cease to exist. As your Self is bodiless, the fear of death, the fear of decay, etc., ceases. As the Self is world-less, the fear of anything else happening, to you or for you, ceases. As the Self is eternal, the fear of going out of existence is laughably absurd. As the Self is infinite, the fear of being bounded or limited in any way vanishes. Fear in any form vanishes by plunging into the Knowledge of the Self. This is the boundless sea of perfect bliss. You are invited to dive in.

> **Annamalai, the Transcendental One,**
> **That is the Eye behind the eye of the mind,**
> **Which eye and other senses cognize[s],**
> **Which in their turn illuminate the sky (space)**
> **And all the other elements as well,**
> **That is again the Spirit-sky (space) in which**

**The mind-sky (space) does appear; That
    shines within
The Heart which is of every thought quite free
And with gaze fixed within remains fixed as That;
Annamalai (Arunachala), the self-effulgent, shines.
But Grace is needed most. So, faithful be
Unto the Self and Bliss will then result.**

The absolute Arunachala has no top and no bottom. No one has ever found its beginning; no one will find its end. It is the self-effulgent, infinite Consciousness of rock-like, solid Existence. It is that which is the transcendental One. That is the Self within you, which is never touched by anything. **That is the Eye behind the eye of the mind,** which cognizes the other senses. To sense, to see etc., the world, is to illuminate the elements. The mind sees the senses. What sees the mind?

The elements are not forever. The senses are certainly not eternal. The mind is not immortal. That which is the "eye" referred to here has no beginning and no end. It is unborn and imperishable. It is the one that knows. There is no other knower. Within the mind-space, the space of this universe is contained. Within what great space does the bubble of the mind-space appear? That great space is the infinite Consciousness. Within that alone appears the mind, which is but an imagined bubble. Within that bubble appears the imagined world. You are of the nature of this infinite space of Consciousness. Make no mistake about it.

That shines within the Heart, which is of every thought quite free, and, with gaze fixed within, remains as That. Fix your gaze upon the realization of That, the true Self. Fix your gaze upon the very quintessence of your being. Do not misidentify with whatever is conceived in thought. Then, That shines. The Consciousness shines for itself. Grace is needed most, and it is already present in boundless abundance. We are not lacking in anything. To realize the perfect fullness of this grace, be faithful. To what should you be faithful? Unto the Self, which is not a body, certainly not an ego, but that one, self-luminous, ever-existent Self. Have faith in that, inquire and become convinced that that alone is your nature. If you practice in this manner, if you deeply inquire in this way, what will be the result? He has declared it: Bliss.

IV
August, 2013

Om Namo Bhagavate Sri Ramanaya

The grace of Bhagavan is infinite and eternal. Like space, it is all-encompassing. Like air, it refreshes the life. Like fire, it illuminates. Like water, it dissolves. Like earth, it supports. With his grace, he has bestowed invaluable spiritual instruction, revealing the Reality of the Self and the means to realize it.

This Realization of the Self is of the utmost importance. Whatever else may be done in life or may be left undone, it is essential to realize the Truth of the Self, for it is by that alone that there is lasting peace and complete happiness. If the Truth of the Self is not realized, what is the good of anything else? Thus, to realize the Self is the supreme attainment, the highest good, and the fulfillment of the purpose of life.

We are exceedingly blessed, because we have his instruction, his grace, and his example. He said that what he realized is realizable by all. Because this is his word, there can be no doubt about it. In addition, if Self-Realization pertained to the individual, doubts could arise as to whether or not I can realize. Since, though, the revelation of the Truth of the Self lies precisely in the nonexistence of an ego, or the individual, there is no scope for the doubt, "Can I realize or not?" Relying on his grace and penetrating deeply within with the guidance of the spiritual instruction, Realization is certain. How can Realization be certain? It is because the Reality is certain. How is the revelation of the Reality to come about? It is by the Knowledge of one's Self, Atma-Vidya, Self-Knowledge.

How spiritually glorious is his state, beyond all worldly accomplishment, an ocean of peace, eternal bliss, and perfection. It is that which is lauded in all of the scriptures. Its depth and greatness are ineffable. In the attempt to describe it, words and thoughts turn back, unable to grasp. We can say that it is the Infinite and the Eternal, but what does that really mean? It is inconceivable, but is realizable; for he said that what he realized is certainly realizable by all. Consider the vastness of that which is revealed by the spiritual instruction. Consider deeply and thoroughly the importance of Self-Realization. Let the recognition of the importance of it come with the necessary one-pointed dedication turned inward to realize. This is essential. Contemplate this.

Self-Realization is not a bodily state. Indeed, it is freedom from bodily states entirely. Self-Realization is not a sensory state. Indeed, it is utter transcendence of the senses. Self-Realization is not a mental state. Indeed, in this Realization, the mind is nonexistent. Self-Realization does not pertain to an individual. Indeed, when the false assumption of individuality subsides, then and there shines the revelation of the Truth of the Self. Self-Realization is Self-Knowledge; not mere perception, not mere conception, but true Knowledge. It is Knowledge of the Self, by the Self. Indeed, it is that Knowledge in which Being and Knowing are identical. It is that Knowledge in which the threefold division of knower, knowing, and known is not so. It is the comprehension of Reality, by Reality. You are this Reality, the one solitary Existence. You have only to know yourself as you truly are.

About this Self-Knowledge, Atma-vidya, Sri Bhagavan instructs,

> **Self-Knowledge is an easy thing,**
> **The easiest thing there is.**
> **The Self is something that is entirely real**
> **Even for the most ordinary man;**
> **It could be said that a clear gooseberry**
> **Is an illusion by comparison.**

Self-Knowledge is an easy thing, the easiest thing there is. What would be the easiest thing there is? To be this easy, it would have to be already existent. Indeed, to be the easiest thing there is, it would have to be ever-existent. What is ever-existent? Thoughts and things are transitory. What is ever-existent? Inquire, discriminate within, what is ever-existent. This is spiritual instruction for you and about you and truly by you. What within you, what about you, is ever-existent? This means that it has no beginning, no end, and no interruption. Not even for a moment can it cease to exist. What is that?

Awareness, which is Being, is ever-existent. **Self-Knowledge is the easiest thing there is.** Upon profound inquiry as to the nature of the Self, the state of Self-Knowledge is found to alone exist and ignorance not at all. Ignorance is not a real state. Knowledge is the true state, the only state that there actually is. If the ignorant belief in the existence of the individual, who is the possessor of the ignorance, subsides through clear inquiry, Knowledge is found to be identical with Being. The ever-existent Self's Knowledge of itself is referred to here. If you think that Self-Knowledge will begin in the future, that Self-Realization will be attained in the future, this supposes an individual for whom such would occur and for whom the present state is ignorance. But is the individual real? Are you an individual? If the individual, or ego, were real, Self-Knowledge would be a difficult thing, indeed, the most difficult thing in the world. Since the individual is not the reality, he says, **Self-Knowledge is an easy thing, the easiest thing** that **there is.** For the ego, being unreal, Knowledge is impossible. For the Self that you truly are, ignorance is impossible. Between the Real and the unreal there is no dichotomy, no division, for the Real alone exists, and the unreal does not exist at all. Because this is so he says, **Self-Knowledge is an easy thing, the easiest thing there is.** Because it is ever-existent, the Self, which is the Knowledge, is the easiest thing there is. Just as there is no alternative to Existence, likewise is it with this Knowledge.

The Self is utterly nonobjective. The Self can never become an object apart from you, so that you could know it as an "it," or a "this." If the Self were an object, there might be difficulty in the attainment of it, but, since the Self is nonobjective and the Knowledge must necessarily be nonobjective in order to realize it, he says, it is the easiest thing that there is. That which is objective comes and goes. The nonobjective is forever and is without beginning or end. The nonobjective is the ever-existent. Being ever-existent and not an object to be attained or lost, Self-Knowledge is the easiest thing that there is.

All of one's efforts in spiritual practice are directed toward the destruction of delusion. The Reality, itself, requires no effort. The Knowledge of the Self, being one with the Self, is likewise. Of course, we casually speak of putting forth one's best effort and persevering to realize the Self, but the efforts are actually directed toward the abandonment of ignorance and the destruction of delusion. That which remains shines as true Knowledge, your real Being. Hence, he says, it is the easiest thing that there is.

Ever-existent, the nonobjective, and the indestructible remainder when everything else has been negated through clear inquiry is Self-Knowledge. He says, **The Self is something that is entirely real even for the most ordinary man.** The Self is your very Being. Can there ever be any doubt regarding your Existence? It is plainly self-evident. There is no one who is not the Self. **It could be said that a clear gooseberry is an illusion by comparison.** The gooseberry in the palm of one's hand refers to the self-evident nature, to something plainly obvious. So it is with Existence. What you may assume is plainly evident, your sense perceptions, are not so. They are illusory. What is plainly evident is that you exist. The attributes associated with such existence are illusory; the conceived, embodied, etc. are illusions. Just Existence by itself is entirely real.

Only from the mind's perspective of an existent state of dualism, or ignorance, can there be the corollary conception of the attainment of Self-Realization. As the mind is recognized to be utterly nonexistent, how could its doubts survive? One realizes that there are not two states, an ignorant state and a realized state, for the ignorant state does not actually exist, and what is called "the realized state" is actually just Existence as it is, pure Consciousness.

Do you make any effort to exist? Do you make any effort to know? To think of something requires a deliberate effort. As for that which knows thoughts as well as the absence of thoughts, the knowing that is continuous and ever-existent, do you need to do anything in order to make it be? What is to be realized is that your identity is only this Existence, this Consciousness which is Knowledge. Truly, it is only from the clarity regarding one's identity that you can understand why the Maharshi declared that it is the easiest thing there is.

What could possibly be more clearly evident than one's own Existence? It is uncaused, not produced, and never lost. What do you associate with the Existence, which is not actually the Existence? Discriminate clearly the ever-existent from the transitory, the Self from what is objective. Self-Knowledge is the easiest thing because it is innate, of the nature of pure Consciousness. So, then, can the destruction of ignorance be difficult? As soon as one discerns ignorance as ignorance, there is found to be no difficulty whatsoever in the abandonment of it. To perceive ignorance as ignorance, a misidentification as a misidentification, is alone necessary. The ability to so discriminate is innate, even for the most ordinary person.

Indeed, so much is this so that the conceptions of difficult and easy do not really apply. The Self exists, forever shining in its own Light, and you are that. Just as certain as you are of your Existence, just so certain you should be of your identity as the Existence alone.

In your practice, eliminate the various concepts or tendencies and the one who supposedly possesses them. If you attempt to eliminate the tendencies but leave the ego intact, the tendencies will never be totally gone. On the other hand, if you wish to eliminate the ego but leave the tendencies intact, what kind of freedom would that be? It would be shallow. So, be thorough, be deep.

The actual experience of the Infinite and the Eternal is egoless. For this reason, affirmation is never needed. You need not affirm that you exist; you need only deeply know what the existence is.

The conception of a mind, a distinct, separate, knowing entity, something different than the infinite Consciousness, is the identical concept of an ego. Whether we refer to it as the mind or as the ego or by any other term, it is not the reality. It will not realize its own unreality. It is unreal; it cannot realize anything at all. Similarly, the mind will not think its way out of existence, but there is no necessity for that. Inquiry, which is pure Knowledge, pure Consciousness by nature, by its light, reveals the nonexistence of an ego or mind.

How does a mental issue start? Because it cannot come out of nothing, for something does not come out of nothing, you have to say that it comes out of the Consciousness, or the Existence. Since the Existence, or the Consciousness, is forever unmodified, what can we say comes out of it? All that we can say is, "The Real ever is; the unreal never is." The Real alone knows that.

Bhagavan says,

The Self, which shines as the Sun within the Heart,
Is real and all-pervading. It will reveal
Itself as soon as false thought is destroyed
And not one speck remains. For this thought is
The cause of the appearance of false forms,
The body and the world, which seem to be
Real things in spite of the Self, which
      steadfast stands,
The ever-changeless, firm as Truth, itself.
When the Self shines forth, darkness will be
      dispersed,
Afflictions cease, and Bliss alone remain.

"Heart" means the quintessence of your Being. There is nothing more interior to it. It is the within-ness itself. **The Sun** that shines **within the Heart** means the nature of this quintessential Being is luminous Consciousness. This Being-Consciousness is also Bliss, but, if it is unknown, the Bliss appears as if hidden. Being is mistaken for the existence of various things, and Consciousness, or true Knowledge, is considered a conception, thought and such. The Self, though, is this Being-Consciousness, **the Sun within the Heart.** This, he declares, **is real and all-pervading.** Reality can only be One. Multiplicity, or division, is a product of imagination. If we imagine Reality to be multiple, those multiple realities depend on the perceiver thereof. What is the nature of the perceiver? Inquiring in this way, the individual perceiver and the false sense of multiplicity both vanish, because they are not real. The singular, indivisible Reality remains, shining, like the sun, as one's quintessential Being, the Heart.

The Self **is real and all-pervading.** The Existence that is omnipresent is your existence. Particularization, or distinction from it, is due only to misidentification and is not, in fact, real. The Consciousness, which is your true Being, is real and is all-pervading. Is there any experience you have at any time that is outside of Consciousness, or apart from Consciousness? No matter how small or subtle, or how large and gross, the experience seems to be the Consciousness is there. You never have any experience apart from it, or outside of it. This Consciousness is the Reality. This all-pervasive Consciousness is what you are; so it is called "the Self." If it is truly all-pervading, there is nothing distinct from it to be pervaded. Division, or difference, is a result of imagination and is never actually the fact. What is real? The Being-Consciousness, which is the Self.

If Being-Consciousness, infinite and eternal, is the Self and if this alone is real and all-pervading, so that there is nothing anywhere outside of it or apart from it,—no separate individual, no separate universe, and no separate God—why is it not experienced as such? If it alone is the Reality, why are other things apparently experienced and why does it seem to be hidden? **It,** meaning the Self, the pure Being-Consciousness, **will reveal itself as soon as false thought is destroyed and not one speck remains.** How will It reveal itself if thought is destroyed? Consciousness is naturally self-luminous. It does not require the instrumentality of thought to know itself. True Knowledge is not thought-dependent. It is of the very nature of this innermost Consciousness. What produces multiplicity or division? It is only thought, imagination. If this thought, or imagination, can be destroyed, differentiation, being unreal, will vanish, and the solitary Reality alone will remain, in the Knowledge of itself. False thought should be destroyed. How do you destroy it? The destruction is by seeing its falsity. Ignorance is destroyed by true Knowledge alone. Inherent in true Knowledge is the recognition of the false or unreal as actually false and unreal. How unreal is the unreal? It is completely so. How real is the Real? It is completely so. To know the Truth, this should be one's conviction. If you think in terms of partially real and partially unreal, either about the Self or about all other things, this is just more thinking. Existence-Consciousness, or Reality, is entirely itself and is not partially one thing and partially another. If a thought is false, it is entirely so and should be viewed as such.

False thought is destroyed and not one speck remains, not even the subtlest notion of "I," the thinker. Consider your thoughts; which one of them is a false thought? Are any of them the Truth? Are any of them actually the Consciousness, **the Sun within the Heart**? Some thoughts may appear to have more verity than others, according to other thoughts that measure them, but what thought actually defines the Reality? Existence is not confined or defined by thought. Consciousness is not known by thought. All of the thoughts deal with the unreal. Indeed, the unreal is only a thought. How is thought false? It cannot show you the Reality. How else is it false? It is momentary, appearing only in the waking and dreaming states and disappearing entirely in deep dreamless sleep. As a characteristic of being real is to be ever-existent, thought cannot be so. Indeed, how do you know about any thought, apart from the Consciousness that knows it? Consciousness, though, is without duality and without modification. So, thought is entirely false. Both its content, which is the object of thought, and the idea that thought is existent are false. Thoughts are not real things, and they do not tell you about Reality.

When, through inner discrimination, one determines that thought is false, and thought is negated thereby, what remains is the Self, which is thought-transcendent. It stands revealed. It is not revealed to someone apart from it. It is revealed to itself, and the Self is what you are. To imagine that you are caught within thought, or that you are a thought-entity, or that you are composed of a collection of thoughts—any such definition is entirely false. Let not a trace of that remain, and then see what is real. "And then what is there?"

For the full revelation of the Self just as it is, absolute Knowledge, not one speck remains; not the thought of "I," not a thought of "this." There is a cessation of the misidentification with the thought and the belief that thought is existent. The belief that thought is existent is from the misidentified position of the perceiver thereof, or the conceiver.

Do you ever experience anything outside of Consciousness? If all is within Consciousness, it must be of the very same substance as Consciousness. What is the substance of Consciousness? Is it an "I," a "this," thoughts, things, or is it entirely formless? It must be homogeneous, for if it were divided into parts within itself, it would be destructible. The indestructible, the changeless, alone should be regarded as real. If something could divide Consciousness, so that Consciousness would lose its nature, it would mean that Consciousness would be destructible, and whatever could so divide it would be more powerful than it and would have to be more interior to it. Is there anything more interior than Consciousness?

If, practicing inquiry, you cease to misidentify with thought, seeing the nonexistence of thought will happen of itself. Because the Self is actually the Reality, you need merely discriminate how the thoughts are not you. If they are not you, they are not real. A bundle of falseness is not any truer than a single speck of the false. So, many thoughts are not more substantial than a single thought.

Continuity is borrowed. Just as the existence is borrowed, the identity is borrowed. Let all of that return to its original source. The source is the Being-Consciousness that you are. If thoughts are real and continuous, let them stand up on their own. If, being free of misidentification, you cease to conceive them, see if they appear.

For this thought is the cause of the appearance of false forms, the body and the world, which seem to be real things in spite of the Self, which stands steadfast, the ever-changeless, firm as Truth, itself. In deep sleep, no thought appears, and what form does your experience have? There is no world in deep sleep. There is no body or any other thing. If these things were real, they should always be real. What is it that is always, standing **firm as Truth, itself**? That which is ever-changeless, is the Self, and that is the Reality. It is only because of thought that the body and the world appear and are presumed to be real. They appear as real things, even though they are not real. The existence, or the real quality, is borrowed, as it were. The borrower is mere delusion. One should demand repayment.

In the previous verse, he said that the Self is something that is entirely real, even for the most ordinary person. So, how can one say that the Self is not experienced? On the other hand, as long as there are thoughts, of various kinds or even one speck, the Reality is not known as it is. What one thinks his experiences of it is is a partial view or an illusion.

A mixture of the real and the unreal is the very definition in the scriptures of ignorance. Is the identity of the one who has a partial understanding also partial, a mixture? How can something be partially real and partially unreal?

There is a mix-up, and a mix-up is having a mix-up. Discussing the experience of it is going into great detail about the nature of the waves of a mirage. The mirage water is false; so the waves are also. A description of the waves will not tell you what the underlying reality is.

All this is said in view of discrimination of the absolute Self as it is. We are not discussing here, now, partial advancement or progress in spirituality. If there is greater peace, greater freedom, greater happiness, progress is occurring. If we are speaking about the Self shining forth, in a state of self-luminous, absolute Knowledge, not one speck of false thought can remain.

The Self is real and all-pervading. There cannot be a second or anything other anywhere, not even so much as a thought of it. In thought alone, thought seems to exist. An illusion having an illusion; how could that be? It is not real.

When we come to know the substance as it is, we find that the substance is the Knowledge and there is nothing else whatsoever. There is no one in ignorance and no state of ignorance. The Reality is itself the substance of the realized Knowledge. Hence, it is **the easiest thing there is.**

Thought appears in the waking and dreaming states, and the body and the world appear. Further, one identifies with them, thinking, "I am this body in this world, with a role to play in this world" and so forth and so on. They seem to be real things, but they are not real. Which body and which world seems real? It is according to the state of mind prevailing. In the waking state, the waking body and world seem to be real. In the dreaming state, the dream body and world seem to be real. In the waking state it seems quite obvious that the dream body and world are not true. In the dreaming state, you do not have a thought of the waking body and waking world. The state of mind makes up the entirety of the experience of such a world and such a body; they are changeful appearances according to the state of mind.

Your Existence remains unchanging, **firm as Truth, itself.** Inquire within as to what this unchanging Existence is. It is not to be defined by thought. This refers to interior, thought-free Knowledge of the unchanging Existence. Worlds change. The content of the world changes, and the actual worlds change. Bodies change. The characteristics of the body change, and the actual bodies change over time. What does not change? A world is created; a body is born. What does not change? A world is destroyed; a body dies. What does not change? The world is recreated; a new body is born. What does not change? This could go on for seemingly endless time, yet something remains unchanging. What is this unchanging Existence? The unchanging Existence alone is what you are. To consider yourself to be a body in a world is but a changeful, false thought. To consider yourself to be worldly or embodied is also just a false thought.

That which is being revealed here, the focus of the instruction, is something everyone has and is. It is overlooked, as it were. When you inquire as to what is the position from which you overlook, the overlooking is gone.

The Self is **ever-changeless, firm as Truth, itself.** It never swerves from its own nature. Realized Knowledge is such unswerving abidance and is ever-changeless.

Where true Knowledge is, thought is superfluous. Where there is true Knowledge, thought cannot add anything to it. A thought cannot subtract from it. It is transcendent. Inquiry is composed of such true Knowledge. It is interior Knowledge. It is within you.

In actual inquiry, thought is not involved. The Knowledge of your bodiless Existence does not depend on thinking about it. Obviously, the body does not appear to another body. If we ask for whom the body appears, it must appear for someone who is bodiless. The waking state of mind creates the body. But the waking state of mind does not create your Existence. Bhagavan reveals the Existence that is absolutely bodiless and instructs you to abide firmly in That, as That.

To say that you are the bodiless perceiver of the body is only part way there. It is a definite step in the right direction, but pursue the inquiry further. You will find that you are not a perceiver either. If you were a perceiver of the body, you should always be a perceiver of such; but that is not the experience. But there is always Existence.

Moreover, the perceiver in the waking state must be endowed, at least mentally, with the five senses, in order to perceive the body. The five senses are not with you all of the time. So, your nature must be something else. It is something changeless, something that remains unswervingly and firmly itself and does not change its nature at any time.

Find out if you are a thinker. If you are a thinker, in truth, you should always be a thinker, but you are not. If you have difficulty reaching the thoughtless state, it is because you view it as a state. It is your nature that is being spoken of, not a state that occurs to you. If it is a state that occurs to you, it will come and go. Sometimes, there will be thoughts and sometimes not. Then, within that state of thought, you will look for a cause thereof. Some consider the cause to be mental. Some regard the cause to be physical, even though what is physical is but a product of thinking, regarding appearances within the mind as if they were responsible for the mind. But your nature is something otherwise. If you make your vision nonobjective, focusing on who you are, rather than whatever state appears and comes and goes, what is said about freedom from thought will make much better sense to you.

When the Self shines forth, darkness will be dispersed, afflictions cease, and Bliss alone remain. If Consciousness, which is the Self, is ever-shining, what is meant by **the Self shines forth,** and to whom does it shine forth? When Consciousness knows itself as such is the shining forth. It knows with its interior, thought-transcendent Knowledge. The **darkness will be dispersed.** The darkness is ignorance, which is composed of misidentification. In the context of the misidentification of Bliss, it refers to attachment. How is it dispersed? It is dispersed by the Self shining forth. The power of Knowledge is the power of Consciousness. It is the power of the Self. Nothing else has the power to destroy ignorance. Self-Knowledge alone destroys the darkness of ignorance, and, as ignorance is the cause of affliction, or suffering, such Knowledge alone is liberation from all kinds of suffering. For one who has realized the Self, nothing of the world or of the body and such can cause suffering. Why? It is because the world, the body, and such are but false thought-forms. For one for whom the Self shines forth, not one speck of false thought remains; there is no misidentification. The very cause of suffering, the ignorance of misidentification, is utterly consumed in the fire of Knowledge. What remains?

Bliss alone remain(s). The Self is Bliss. Bliss is identical with Being-Consciousness. Sat-Chit-Ananda (Saccidananda), Being-Consciousness-Bliss, is a threefold term for one indivisible Reality. If Being is not known as it is and there is misidentification as an ego, as a body, and such, Bliss seems to be hidden. If Consciousness is not known and, instead, thought is assumed to be real, the Bliss seems to be hidden. Find your Being, realize the Consciousness as it is, and Bliss is found. There is no alternative to it. It is invariable happiness, and there does not remain an entity separate from it to be an experiencer thereof. Bliss is not insentient; Bliss is identical with Consciousness. Consciousness knowing itself, Being reposing as itself, is Bliss experiencing itself directly, without intermediary.

Bhagavan says,

**The thought "I am the body" is the string
On which are threaded diverse thoughts like beads.
Therefore, on diving deep upon the quest
"Who am I and from where (whence)?" thoughts
        disappear,
And Consciousness of the Self then flashes forth
As the "I-I" within the cavity
Of every seeker's Heart, and this is Heaven,
This is that Stillness, the abode of Bliss.**

How many of your thoughts are based on the supposition of being a body or an embodied entity? The diverse thoughts about ever so many things are like the beads. The string connecting them is this "I am the body" misconception. If you are, in truth, not the body, but you conceive of the idea, "I am the body," what can we say of all the thoughts that proceed based upon that conception? They are as false as their basic premise. The basic premise is that the Self is the body. Are we bodies? "I live," "I die," "I do," "I am of such a size and shape," "I have these various qualities and attributes," "the world surrounds me;" all these are based on the "I am the body" misconception. Without this misconception, what ignorant ideas would be left?

Since the Self shines forth in blissful Self-Knowledge as soon as the misidentification with false thought is destroyed, and since the fundamental misidentification is the "I am the body" misconception, he says, **Therefore, on diving deep upon the quest "Who am I and from where (whence)?" thoughts disappear. Diving deep;** when are you deep? It is when you are below the surface of thought. When you stand unidentified with sensation or with thinking, you are deep. Dive deep. Dive so deep that you find that you have become the depth. For the benefit of the aspirant who considers himself to be outside of the Self, it is said, "Dive deep." When he dives deep, he discovers that he does not have a separate existence, but rather what he thought of himself as diving into, the depth, is what he is. When that is realized, one's vision is nonobjective.

"Who am I?" It is the one question to be answered, but it cannot be answered in words or thoughts. "Who am I?" "I am" is undoubted by anyone. "Who am I?" There is the sense of "I." **Whence;** from where does it spring? It does not come from the body or anything in the body. It does not come from thought. From where does "I" spring? Inquire deeply within, in quest of the "I." It is constant. From where does it come? It cannot come from anything external to you.

On diving deep upon the quest "Who am I and from where (whence)?" thoughts disappear. The thoughts are for you. Who are you? If you properly understand the manner of this inquiry, the objectified portion, which is the thoughts, which are unreal, not the Self, and utterly dependent on the "I" that knows them, disappears. What remains? The **Consciousness of the Self then flashes forth.** It **flashes forth** to itself, not to another, for there are not two selves, one to flash forth and one to see it. **As the "I-I" in the cavity of every seeker's Heart.** Being is only Being, I am only I, not another, such as a thought or a body, but I am only I. What is the meaning of "I"? Aham-Aham, "I"-"I," means "I am I," and that is so changelessly and constantly. The revelation that I am only I and not any "this" is the shining forth of Knowledge, of the nature of Consciousness, for the Self, by the Self. This is nonobjective vision. Where does this Truth flash forth? Within **the cavity of every seeker's Heart.** The space of the Heart is not a physical space. It is said to be the space of the Heart to indicate its formlessness, its all-pervasive nature, its subtlety, and its expansiveness. As all are the Self, anyone, **every seeker,** who turns within in quest of the Self, "Who am I?" searching for the source of "I," realizes this same Truth.

This is Heaven; this is that Stillness, the abode of Bliss. A heaven to which one would go, one would eventually leave. If it is truly heaven, it is within you. To be still is to remain as pure Being. Since Being is always itself, it is the cessation of misidentification by the inquiry "Who am I?" that is referred to as the attainment of stillness, which is to remain in unswerving abidance as the Self, unmoving from the Self. Though the Self is always the Self, in delusion, one thinks that one is separated from it. When the Truth is known by inquiry, stillness is attained; that is, you find yourself to be the unmoving Self. As Being is Bliss, seek your Being, for the sake of your happiness. Happiness, Bliss, depends upon the Realization of the Self.

In relation to the moving, the absolute Existence of the Self is pointed out as being the unmoving. In relation to all that changes, it is spoken of as changeless. All this helps with discrimination, which is essential to the inquiry. Upon Realization of the Self, though, even the attributes qualified as unmoving, unchanging, etc., fall behind; they are not an adequate description.

He equates stillness with Bliss. What is the stillness? That which is indicated is not really one part of a duality. What is absolute stillness? For it to be real, it must be ever-existent. Absolute stillness is not a state attained by the individual. In absolute stillness, the individual and the entire creation have never come to be.

He speaks of the eternal. The cave of the Heart, or the space of the Heart, is pure Consciousness, pure Being. Because it is central, not central in the body, but central to the entire universe that is experienced, it is called the Heart. Because it is most interior, it is called the Heart. It is not a physical sensation and not a physical organ. Likewise, it is not a part or experience of the subtle body.

For changeless, immortal Bliss, you must find that about your nature which is eternal, which has no beginning or ending. It is not something that occurs to you. It is the very nature of you. That which you need to know is found by inquiring, "Who am I?", or "Whence am I?" The effort should be applied in inquiry, "Who am I?" "From where does the sense of 'I' come?" Thus destroy all the false thought, all the misidentification, so that Supreme Bliss, un-intermittent Bliss, permanent Bliss, alone remains and afflictions cease, which means the very possibility of suffering is over, now and forever.

This has nothing to do with moments. Time is but an illusion dreamed in thought. Without a body, without a mind, where is the moment?

Are you not the same in all states? To be without illusion is that stillness. To abide as such, to know yourself as such, is deep meditation.

The inverted lotus analogy appears in the Upanishads. Sri Ramana said it is a specific visualization for those who feel the need to meditate on such. It is not a substitute for the actual inquiry. The reality of the Heart is location-less and bodiless. If it is without location, transcendent even of space, who is to say what is up and down, inverted or right side up? To meet the needs of the temperaments of certain seekers, such imagery, such symbolism, has been devised. You should go to where they point.

Consider the lotus feet of the Sadguru as his manifested form in all of its aspects. The rest of him is so un-manifested that it cannot be described; it is vast beyond measure. By resting oneself at those lotus feet, she finds herself abiding as that which is unspeakable.

> **What is the use of knowing everything**
> **Except the Self? What else is there to know**
> **For anyone when the Self, itself, is known?**
> **On realizing in oneself the Self,**
> **Which is the only self-effulgent One**
> **In myriads of selves, the Light of the Self**
> **Will clearly shine within. This is, indeed,**
> **The true display of Grace, the ego's death,**
> **And the unfolding of the Bliss supreme.**

How can one pass through the entirety of life without knowing himself?

In your experience, you know everything. Everything depends on your knowing of it. Who is the knower thereof? Knowing the knower is most essential. Reality and happiness are the Self. Without knowing the Self, whatever else you may know has no relation to reality or to happiness. If it does not tell you what is and does not provide you with the natural state of happiness, of what use is it?

What else is there to know for anyone when the Self, itself, is known? Knowledge of the Self is Supreme Knowledge. There is nothing higher than that. There is nothing beyond it. When you know your Self, there remains no other existent thing to be known, for the Self alone is real and all-pervading. In the Realization of Supreme Knowledge, there is only One without a second. There is nothing to be known apart from the Knower. The Knower is formless, boundary-less, and everywhere.

For Self-Knowledge to be absolute, it must be as eternal as the Self that is known, which means that it must be identical with it. Is mental attention eternal? True Knowledge constitutes the inquiry. Whose is mental attention? Something sees the mind. The mind does not see it. That which sees the mind, but is unseen by the mind, ought to know itself with its own natural Knowledge. That is truly turning within. In relation to the Self, the mind is external. To look within is to look more deeply than the mind. Mental attention is a faculty or activity of the mind, apparent in two of the three states of mind. It cannot be eternal. It cannot be Self-Knowledge.

Dissolve the mind in the "I" and the "I" in its original nature. There are not two knowers, the Self and the mind. The mind is relatively inert, a collection of thoughts. The movement of attention is something you witness. It is objective to you. It is a faculty of the mind. It is not your Self. The position from which you comprehend this discrimination is not the mind. It is transcendent. You know about that upon which the attention alights, and you know about the attention. Neither of them can be the Knower. Know the Knower.

On realizing in oneself the Self, which is the only Self-effulgent One in myriads of selves, the Light of the Self will clearly shine within. What is it that knows? What is it that illumines? The supposition of a multiplicity of knowers in you, such as the Self, Consciousness, the mind, the intellect, and so forth is based upon misidentification with the mind. A multiplicity of knowers in terms of people, self and others, is based on a misidentification with the body. Stand free of the misidentification with the body and the mind, and you find that there is only one universal Knower. That is Consciousness, and that is your Self. **Self-effulgent** means Self-knowing. Look deeply within; what is it that knows? What is it that knows itself? What is the existence which knows that it exists? It cannot be the body, and it cannot be the mind, which is but a collection of thoughts. Inquire in this manner, and the Light of the Self will clearly shine within.

The shining of Self-Knowledge within by the Light of the Self, for the Light of the Self, one without the least bit of multiplicity, is **the true display of Grace. It is the ego's death and the unfolding of the Bliss supreme.** The idea of a second one, a second knower, a perceiver or experiencer, something other than the Self, is the ego identity. Its death, found by Knowledge alone, is the supreme Bliss. The discovery of such by Knowledge is Grace. The ego has no part in it. This Grace, which may be said to be all around you, is actually within you, and by the ego's subsidence in Knowledge, the Grace is realized. As is the case with the Self, it is inconceivable. Although inconceivable, you can realize it. Such is the purpose of this Atma Vidya, Self-Knowledge.

The Self is the solitary Reality. It alone exists. To know something else is merely imagination. In imagination, one merely knows the unreal. **What else is there to know for anyone, when the Self, itself, is known?** The Self is pure Existence. It is One and undivided. Who is to know something else? **On realizing in oneself the Self, which is the only self-effulgent One in myriads of selves, the Light of the Self will clearly shine within.** The realization of the Self is one of identity. There is only one Self. The Self, of the nature of Being-Consciousness-Bliss, should be realized as your very identity, as the only Self that there actually is. It is the solitary Consciousness, the only knower. If we think of ourselves as multiple, who is it that knows the multiplicity? It is only in the context of misidentification with the mind that one thinks of oneself as if divided, as the Self to be realized and a self to realize. It is only misidentification with the body that gives rise to the belief in multiple individual entities, multiple knowers. There is only one Consciousness, and this is seen clearly by thought-transcendent Knowledge. **This is, indeed, the true display of Grace, the ego's death and the unfolding of the Bliss supreme.** The Grace is ever-existent. That which is ever-existent alone is the Reality. What greater Grace can there be but **the ego's death,** for it is the ending of all suffering and the disappearance of the entire illusion of bondage? The death of the ego is not the death of something real. Only the unreal can be destroyed. The Reality is imperishable, without beginning and without end. This Reality, this Existence-Consciousness, is the Grace. The illusory notion, or false assumption, of an ego is alone the cause of delusive bondage and its consequent suffering. By the subsidence, or destruction, of the illusory ego, the innate Bliss of the Self shines forth clearly. To whom does it shine forth? To itself, for Bliss is not insentient. Bliss is identical with Being-Consciousness, Saccidananda (Sat-chit-ananda).

If you seem to know something else, inquire, "For whom is this?" Seek the nature of the knower. Realizing the quintessence of the knower, you find one undivided Consciousness and that that is the sole existent Reality, the only Self that there is. The Knowledge of the only Self, being the only Self, is the destruction of the ego illusion, and the destruction of that is self-revealed Bliss.

> **In order that the bonds of destiny**
> **And all its kindred may at last be loosed,**
> **And so that one may also be released**
> **From the dread cycle of both birth and death,**
> **This path than others is far easier;**
> **Therefore, be still and keep a silent hold**
> **On tongue and mind and body. That which is**
> **The self-effulgent will arise within.**
> **This is the Supreme Experience. Fear will cease.**
> **This is the boundless sea of perfect Bliss.**

How is one to be liberated from this samsara, the repetitive cycle of illusion, of birth and death? What one does within an illusion does not free one of the illusion. What is necessary, all that is necessary, is transcendent Knowledge, Atma-Vidya—Self-Knowledge. **This path than others is far easier.** Which path? The path of Self-Knowledge, the inquiry to know who you truly are. Why is it easier? The easiest thing there is is the ever-existent, which is also the nonobjective. Such Self-inquiry alone does not take for granted the assumption of individuality, the ego supposition, which is the root of the entire samsara, though it appears as if an experiencer within it. Seek the ever-existent, the nonobjective, within yourself.

Therefore, be still and keep a silent hold on tongue and mind and body. What is stillness? It is to remain unswervingly as your true Existence. Existence, being only One, for the Self is not multiple, who is to swerve? Who separates from the Self? Can such be possible? Therefore, to be still means to abide free of misidentification. It means to remain free of the delusions of "I" and "this." What is this **silent hold on tongue and mind and body?** Bhagavan says, "Silence is that in which no ego-'I' arises." To keep a silent hold is to remain free of the ego notion, whether such is considered in relation to the activities of the body, of speech or communication, or the activities of the mind. Indeed, if you did not misidentify with the body, with speech, and with the mind, what form would the ego have? What would be left of it? Its utter nonexistence would be self-evident.

Remaining free of misidentification, pursuing ardently this easy path of knowing yourself and abiding entirely free of the false assumption of individuality, that which is **the self-effulgent will arise within.** The self-effulgent is Consciousness. It requires no other light to know or to be known. Nothing else is so. Your senses are the known, and your thoughts are the known. They are not the knower. What knows? What shines? That you exist is doubtless. By what light do you know that you exist? Do you require anything else, any kind of instrument such as the senses or the mind, to know that you exist? Existence knows itself, without dependence on anything else whatsoever. The appearance of everything else, which is entirely unreal, does, indeed, depend on the Existence, but the Existence does not depend on anything else. You know all else; all else does not know itself, but you know yourself. What is the nature of this "you"?

The Self-luminous Consciousness shines for itself. **This is the Supreme Experience.** It is the Reality. All other experience is transitory; this is eternal. All other experience depends on a state of mind, waking, dreaming and such. This is mind-transcendent. In truth, it is the only experience, for it is the only existence.

If you appear to have another experience, find out for whom such is. Tracing such inward, all this is reduced to "I." Tracing further inward, inquiring, "Who am I?" the self-effulgent Consciousness is found to be the solitary Existence, the only Reality. Therefore, **fear will cease.** The Upanishad clearly proclaims, "Where there is duality, as it were, there is fear." Where there is no duality, fearlessness is natural. The root of duality is the ego notion.

How many selves are there? There is only one self-effulgent One. To be self-effulgent requires being nonobjective. What is objective is known by another. What is nonobjective is free of another, that is, free of a second. One assumption is piled on top of another. The links are as unreal as the original root.

The ocean of Bliss is immeasurably vast, infinite, and eternal. Who is it that does not experience such? What is his nature? The Self has no ignorance; it has no confusion. If you say that you confuse the Self with the body, the mind and such, who does that? Who is ignorant? The body does not have the ignorance. The thoughts are inert, or, in truth, they are nonexistent. Thoughts seem to be for someone. Who is that someone? He cannot have his origin in that which depends on him, which are the conceptions and perceptions of the mind and body. The real Self is forever unmodified. It never undergoes any change and cannot give birth to anything other than itself. The individual cannot create himself, for that would be absurd. So, what is he, or what is his origin? Your Existence is forever unchanging. If you seek the one who rises up from it and becomes bound in thought and embodied, he will be found to be nonexistent forever.

The revelation of the reality of Being is the revelation of Bliss. Being is Bliss, the same as Consciousness, and, thus, Sat-Chit-Ananda, Being-Consciousness-Bliss. It is a **boundless sea,** which means that you cannot be outside it. It is boundless, and it does not have parts within it, so there is an absence of individuality. Since it is of the nature of Consciousness, there is no one to stand separate from it to say that he experiences it or that he does not experience it. If you want to find absorption in the **boundless sea of perfect Bliss,** the perfect fullness, you must know yourself, what your Existence is. Your Existence cannot be multiple. Multiplicity is a product of imagination and is dependent on thought in order to be conceived. Free of even the least speck of thought is true Knowledge.

Why speak of this in terms of potential? What is the Truth even now? The Truth is eternal. So, it is always so. If it were not always so, ever-existent, it would not be "the easiest path there is."

Who does not know what? Find the nature of "I." You are very certain of your Existence, and the Knowledge of your Existence is inextricable from the Existence itself. How can you say, "I do not know"?

If you think ignorance is real, what do you do to destroy it? If you can perceive ignorance as ignorance, it is destroyed. Only so long as there is not clear discrimination, so that you regard ignorance as true, does it appear to remain. If effort is applied to such destruction of ignorance, and you realize it to be ignorance, casting off all kinds of misidentification, the remainder of pure Knowledge will shine naturally, effortlessly for itself. To attain certainty of Knowledge, just abandon the certainty of ignorance.

When you suppose that Existence will cease to exist, your Self will vanish, there can be fear. When you think that your happiness is to be destroyed, there can be fear. The Existence and the happiness are one and the same. Realizing what Existence is, how it can never cease to exist but always remains unborn, indestructible, unformed, and homogeneous, is to be free of fear. For that, there is neither birth nor death. This alone frees one from the dreaded **cycle of both birth and death.** The **boundless sea of perfect Bliss** is your actual identity, your own Being. Inquire "Who am I?" to know with certainty yourself as That and That alone.

Bhagavan says,

> **Annamalai, the Transcendental One,**
> **That is the Eye behind the eye of the mind,**
> **Which eye and other senses cognize[s],**
> **Which in their turn illuminate the sky (space)**
> **And all the other elements as well,**
> **That is again the Spirit-sky (space) in which**
> **The mind-sky (space) does appear; That**
>   **shines within**
> **The Heart which is of every thought quite free**
> **And with gaze fixed within remains fixed as That;**
> **Annamalai (Arunachala), the self-effulgent, shines.**
> **But Grace is needed most. So, faithful be**
> **Unto the Self and Bliss will then result.**

It is mere delusion when one imagines oneself as an entity within the mind, the mind within the body, and the body within the world. Such is merely an illusion. The entire space of the universe is contained within the mind. This is seen clearly by all those who abandon the misidentification with the body. If misidentification with the body remains, how this is so is incomprehensible. Without misidentification with the body, all is contained within the mind. Everything perceived by the senses and the senses themselves are only in and of the mind. In what is the mind? If all this is in the mind-space, where, or in what, is the mind-space? He says, the Spirit-space, meaning thereby the infinite Consciousness. This infinite Consciousness is transcendental. It is not defined and is certainly not confined by the senses or by the thoughts of the mind.

Where is it to be realized? It **shines within the Heart.** The Heart refers to your quintessential Being, which is from **every thought quite free.** Your Being is innately free from thought. Not a single thought applies to it. Indeed, in That, for That, thought has never come to be. If you know your quintessential Being, which is the Heart, undefined by any thought, including the thought of being a thinker, your gaze is truly **fixed within.** "Within" means nonobjective. It does not mean in the body, in the senses, or in the mind, but it signifies nonobjective. If your gaze is fixed in such a nonobjective manner, you remain as That. That is Brahman, the Reality. Though inconceivable, it is realizable. It is self-effulgent. What is it in you that ever knows, yet remains unknown, as it were? Who is the unknown knower of all that is known? It remains unknown in the sense of being unconceived. Yet it is the best known, self-known, for it is the self-effulgent One.

For this realization, **Grace is needed most.** The need is already fulfilled. Grace is already present. One need be merely keenly aware of it. The power to realize does not lie with an unreal ego or a nonexistent mind. The power to realize is of Grace, yet Grace is of the Self. So, be faithful. To what should you be faithful? To the Self. The Self is the Grace. The Self is the Realization. The Self alone is the Reality. If this is understood, Bliss will then result.

V

Om Namo Bhagavate Sri Ramanaya

Self-Knowledge: what is it? Bhagavan continuously, ever so graciously reveals it. What is it that is so revealed?

We start at the end; the end is the beginning, say the wise. You exist. It is doubtless. Even if you were to entertain a doubt about your existence, you assume your existence is there in order to entertain the doubt. You exist. You are Existence. Existence is not an attribute, and it is not a possession. So, you do not have existence; you are Existence.

How do you know that you exist? You exist, and you know that you exist. How do you know it? It is not dependent on sensation. It does not depend on mental conception. The Existence and Knowledge of Existence are of an undivided nature. What do you suppose this Existence to be, and what is it really? Knowledge of something else contains differences. There are the knower and the thing known. The knowing is the relation between them. Self-Knowledge is otherwise, for you can never become an object to yourself. How do you know that you exist? With or without thought, you exist, and you know that you exist. With or without bodily sensations, you exist, and you know that you exist. The "you" that knows is not different from that which is known.

Realization of the true nature of the Self is rightly regarded as the supreme attainment, for, if you abide in Self-Knowledge, you dwell in lasting peace and happiness. Thus, it is the very goal of life. Realization of this is the highest. Even though it is the supreme, the highest of the highest, Sri Bhagavan says in Atma Vidya that it is an easy thing. The opening verse of *Atma-Vidya* says:

> **Self-Knowledge is an easy thing,**
> **The easiest thing there is.**
> **The Self is something that is entirely real,**
> **Even for the most ordinary man;**

**It could be said that a clear gooseberry
Is an illusion by comparison.**

What is the **easiest thing**? That which is ever-existent is the easiest, for it requires no new attainment. Truly speaking, Self-Knowledge is characterized by an absence of the individual who would claim it as easy or difficult. Regarding your own existence and the innate knowledge of it, is such difficult, is such easy, or do easy and difficult just not apply? That which is self-existent and self-evident, beyond the distinctions of easy and difficult, can be called the easiest thing there is.

What is ever-existent? Certainly your body is not ever-existent, so Self-Knowledge must, therefore, necessarily be bodiless in character. What is ever-existent? Is any thought, any mental mode, or any state of mind, ever-existent? If not, Self-Knowledge must be mind-transcendent. Examine your actual experience; what is ever-existent? Certainly the perception of objects is not. Is individuality ever-existent? If not, Self-Knowledge does not occur for the individual, nor is individuality retained in it. Your existence is ever-existent; it is bodiless, mind-transcendent, ego-less Existence.

The Self is something that is entirely real. Consider deeply what this means. It is not more at one time and less at another. It is entirely real. Your existence is entirely real, and whatever is regarded as other than your existence is unreal. The unreal actually has no existence. He says that this is true, **even for the most ordinary person.** The one Self alone exists, in and as all.

The reference to the **clear gooseberry** is a phrase indicative of something completely, clearly evident. That which is clearly evident to the mind and senses is an illusion in contrast to Self-Knowledge. Self-Knowledge is self-evident. How do you know you exist? Being is Consciousness. Consciousness knows itself; nothing else is so. Consciousness, which is your very Being, knows itself, and it is what it knows. What is your existence? At the very same depth that you know you exist, discern what the existence is.

That which is real is immutable. What in you never changes? That which is real is always so. What in you has neither birth nor death, neither creation nor destruction? When it is asked, "What in you?", what definition is assumed for the "you"? That which is the Self can be only One. What in you is without difference, free of multiplicity, and never divided from itself?

The assumption that there is another kind of self, other than absolute Existence, absolute Consciousness, is delusion. Freedom from such ignorance is Self-Knowledge. Destroy the ignorance, and you find that the Knowledge is ever-existent and not a new attainment. So, while we loosely refer to the attainment of Self-Knowledge, what actually occurs is the destruction of ignorance. This is why he says Self-Knowledge is the easiest thing there is. Remove the superimposed illusion, and the substrate, which is real, stands by itself. As for the destruction of ignorance, what can be difficult about that? Any obstacles encountered are merely imagined, for ignorance is not real. How difficult can it be to destroy something that is not real?

The Self is ever-existent. Knowledge of the Self is of the same nature. If the view is otherwise, such as a mental conception, duality appears. Nondual Knowledge has no alternative. What for you is self-evident? Existence, just Existence; not existing as this or that, but just Existence. The end is the beginning.

> **The Self, which shines as the Sun within the Heart,**
> **Is real and all-pervading. It will reveal**
> **Itself as soon as false thought is destroyed**
> **And not one speck remains. For this thought is**
> **The cause of the appearance of false forms,**
> **The body and the world, which seem to be**
> **Real things in spite of the Self, which**
> > **steadfast stands,**
> **The ever-changeless, firm as Truth, itself.**
> **When the Self shines forth, darkness will be**
> > **dispersed,**
> **Afflictions cease, and Bliss alone remain.**

By **Heart** is meant one's quintessential Being, and **Sun** signifies the self-luminous Consciousness. That is the Self which, self-luminous, shines and which is the essence of all essences, interior to which there is nothing else. Being of the nature of Existence-Consciousness, it is indivisible, unchanging, formless, and undifferentiated. That is **real and all-pervading.** Real is that which actually exists; it does not appear but exists. If something is all-pervading, truly all-pervading, there remains no more distinction between that which pervades and the pervaded. There is no scope left for the pervaded to exist at all, except as the pervader. This is the Self. Not any particularized thing is the Self, but the Reality, which is all-pervasive, is the Self.

If you regard yourself solely as the real and all-pervasive One, what is your experience? If the Self is real and all-pervasive, so as to be One without a second, why is it that it is not experienced as such? It is due only to ignorance prevailing. Ignorance does not alter the Reality. It merely makes the unreal appear as real and the Real as if unreal. If ignorance is removed, the Self shines, self-revealed.

It will reveal itself as soon as false thought is destroyed and not one speck remains. What is false thought? Every thought mistaken to be you who are the Reality, the all-pervasive, self-luminous Self alone, is false. Any thought with which you misidentify is false. Any thought, the content of which you mistake to be real, is false. The idea that there is such an existent thing called "thought" is also false. Because it is false, it can be destroyed. If it were real, to any extent, it would never be destroyed, for the real always is. What destroys false thought? Knowledge, in the form of inquiry, does so. The inquiry that discerns Reality shines by the light of Reality, itself. That is **the Sun within the Heart,** the source of all wisdom. So, first, disidentify from all thought. Cease to regard the content of thought as real, and, then, knowing the nature of the Self, cease to regard thought as anything existent. When ignorance is destroyed by Knowledge, nothing real is actually destroyed, but ignorance vanishes, having been known as ignorance, and its effects, the illusion of bondage and consequent suffering, are no more.

This thought is the cause of the appearance of false forms, the body and the world, which seem to be real things in spite of the Self, which steadfast stands, the ever-changeless, firm as Truth, itself. When thought is active, such as in the waking and dreaming states, forms become apparent. They may be gross or they may be subtle, but they are just forms of thought. What you regard as gross form is of the same nature as what is regarded as subtle form. Consider the case of a dream. In a dream, you are endowed with dream perception and dream conception. The concepts you regard as more internal, the percepts as external. Regarding perceiving objects in the dream, from the vantage point of the waking state, you know that all of that—the subject and the object, the subtle and the gross, the interior and the exterior—is just a dream, just your thought. The waking state is very similar. With **the appearance of false forms, the body and the world,** illusion seems to hold sway.

In the waking and dreaming states, a body appears. If you are endowed with a body, a world appears. In deep dreamless sleep, in the absence of thought activity, no body appears, and no world appears. What appears and disappears cannot be the Reality. The Reality is the Self, which despite that illusory play, remains **steadfast, the ever-changeless, firm as Truth, itself.** Regard only that which is changeless as real. That which changes is unreal. Changefulness is not the definition of unreal; it is characteristic of the unreal. The unreal is completely unreal. A body appears, and a body disappears, whether due to changes of states of mind or changes of incarnation. A world appears, and a world disappears; this can be due to changes of mind or to cosmic dissolution. All the while, there is something unchanging, unmoving, that neither appears nor disappears. That which is so is alone yourself. To assume otherwise is merely to become entangled in false thought.

When the Self shines forth, darkness will be dispersed, afflictions cease, and Bliss alone remain. When does the Self shine forth? In reality, it always does; it is invariable. When the darkness of ignorance is destroyed, then, it is said that the Self shines forth. What is it that destroys the darkness? That, also, is the Self shining forth. Although one normally expects the causality to be ignorance is destroyed and the Self shines forth, in this verse, Sri Bhagavan has reversed the causality, and the Self shines forth and ignorance or **darkness** is **dispersed,** thus showing that the liberating power of Self-Knowledge is inherent in the Self. It is the sole power that destroys delusion. **Affliction ceases.** How is it so? From misidentification comes the idea of being bound. From bondage comes suffering. To be free of suffering, liberate yourself from the imagined bondage. To liberate yourself from the imagined bondage, cease to misidentify. To cease to misidentify, you have only to inquire deeply, profoundly, "Who am I?" In the self-luminous, nonobjective Knowledge of the Self, suffering becomes impossible. With the ending of suffering, what remains? **Bliss alone,** he says. This and all the remainder of the verses conclude with Bliss. Our very Being, of the nature of the inner self-luminous Consciousness, is Bliss. Bliss does not come to one, no more than Being comes to one. We may say that it wells up from within, but, upon the dissolution of false thought, all ideas of "this" and "I" gone, it simply shines; it simply is itself. What you are is Existence, what you are is Consciousness, and what you are is Bliss. These three, Being-Consciousness-Bliss, are not attributes or qualities. They are what you are. Although the description is threefold, Being-Consciousness-Bliss, Sat-Chit-Ananda, what is indicated thereby is only, absolutely One.

Cease to regard the world as being real in any respect whatsoever. Abandon any tendency to misidentify with the body. No longer be fooled by the play of your own thought, but know it is false, and you, yourself, will shine forth, to yourself, by yourself. The Reality realizes, or comprehends, itself. Dive inward, inquiring, "Who am I?"

> **The thought "I am the body" is the string**
> **On which are threaded diverse thoughts like beads.**
> **Therefore, on diving deep upon the quest**
> **"Who am I and from where (whence)?" thoughts**
> **   disappear,**
> **And Consciousness of the Self then flashes forth**
> **As the "I-I" within the cavity**

Of every seeker's Heart, and this is Heaven,
This is that Stillness, the abode of Bliss.

Consider your own mind; how much of the content of it is based on the idea, the supposition, "I am the body"? To how many thoughts is this integral? If that supposition were absent, what would your mind be? **Diverse thoughts** are **like beads.** The **thread** running through them is the assumption, "I am the body." If the notion "I am the body" were removed from the sense of "I," what would remain?

Because the diverse thoughts depend on the "I am the body" misidentification, **therefore, on diving deep upon the quest "Who am I and from where (whence)?" thoughts disappear,** They vanish because they are unreal. Dive deep in the interior quest, "Who am I?" It is only because this is not questioned that samsara appears. If one inquires, samsara disappears. "Who am I and from where?" That is, from where does the sense of "I" derive? It does not come from the exterior world, which is considered exterior only in relation to the body. The world does not give you your sense of "I;" it certainly does not give you the Self. From where does the sense of "I" come? Certainly it does not come from the body. After all, the body is for the "I," the "I" is not for the body. **From where?** "Where," in this case, does not mean a location. The idea of location is just one of those beads on the thread of "I am the body." From where does your sense of "I" come? Trace inwardly. Whether you inquire "Who am I?" or "Whence am I?" the answer will be the same. The answer is the nature of the inquirer. Pose the question deeply to yourself, "Who am I?" and trace the sense of "I" to its source. If you inquire in this manner, thoughts regarding yourself or anything other disappear. What remains is unalloyed Consciousness that shines forever, that shines now, that always shines. Consciousness is itself the Knowledge.

Upon inquiring, "Who am I?" or "From where am I?" thoughts disappear. They cease to be regarded as true. They cease to be regarded as existent entities. **The Consciousness of the Self then flashes forth,** for Consciousness is Knowledge. This is Self-Knowledge, not knowing of something else, but Self-Knowledge, in which the Self is known by itself, for itself.

Such Knowledge or **Consciousness of the Self flashes forth as the "I-I" within the cavity of every seeker's Heart.** "I-I" is a phrase that appears in *Ribhu Gita* and throughout the Maharshi's teachings. What does it mean? I am "I," and not other; no "this," just "I." Regarding all of "this," "neti neti, not this, not this," is the conclusion. What you are is only "I," only the Self. You realize that you have never become an individual or anything other than the Self. To realize this, inquire deeply, thoroughly, "Who am I?"

Where is this realization? **In the cavity,** or we could say space, **of every seeker's Heart.** It is like space because of its all-pervasive nature. It is like space because it has no shape, and it has no boundary. It is like space because it is indivisible. It is your quintessential Being.

Just "I," just the quintessential Being, just the self-luminous Consciousness, is indicated by **Heaven.** Heaven is where God dwells, is it not? Where does God dwell? As the Self of all beings, the beginning, middle, and end of all beings. If you see yourself as you are, God sees God as God is. What is God? To find out, you had better know yourself.

This is that Stillness, the abode of Bliss. Stillness is found in that which is ever the same. What in you is changelessly the same? What is it that does not move when thought moves? When thought moves, where does it move? Perhaps, it does not really move at all. Stillness is transcendence of all name and form. Regard name as the conceivable; form is the perceptible. Stillness is absolute transcendence of all such. **This is that Stillness.** It is not bodily stillness. Now, the body moves. Later, the body will be quite still. The stillness that is spoken of here is of an absolute, spiritual nature. It is supreme peace, and it is immeasurable Bliss, uncaused, unconditioned happiness. It is Bliss that is One with Being.

> **What is the use of knowing everything**
> **Except the Self? What else is there to know**
> **For anyone when the Self, itself, is known?**
> **On realizing in oneself the Self,**
> **Which is the only self-effulgent One**
> **In myriads of selves, the Light of the Self**

Will clearly shine within. This is, indeed,
The true display of Grace, the ego's death,
And the unfolding of the Bliss supreme.

What is the use of knowing everything except the Self? Always in life, you search for happiness. Can knowledge of anything else, except the Self, deliver that happiness? Knowledge of the Self reveals the happiness to be innate. Self-Knowledge is the only way to recover the supreme Bliss, which was never actually lost. Always, you seek to know what is real. Without Self-Knowledge, can Reality be known? Without Knowledge of your very Existence, how would the existence of anything else be known? And, if one knows only that which is nonexistent, what good is it? Always, you are intuitively searching for your identity. Without actually inquiring and truly knowing the Self, clearly as you are, but knowing anything else, what good is that? **What is the use of knowing everything except the Self?**

What else is there to know for anyone, when the Self, itself, is known? There is neither an object to be known nor a second kind of knowing nor a second self to be a knower. When "I" is assumed, there is a "this" to be known. When the individual "I" subsides, what else is there to be known? Other than the self-luminous Consciousness, can there really be a second knower, some source of knowledge? If something appears to be known, which is the world, the objectified sphere of experience, inquire, "For whom is it?" or, "By whom is it known?" The reality, the identity, and the happiness will thereby return to their rightful place, their origin. If the individualized perceiver is no longer mistaken to be the Self but is known as a mere supposition, the barest of delusions, there remains nothing else to be perceived. One vast, undifferentiated Being-Consciousness-Bliss exists; it is One, without another, without an alternative. **What else is there to know for anyone, when the Self, itself, is known?**

On realizing in oneself the Self, which is the only self-effulgent One in myriads of selves, the Light of the Self will clearly shine within. How many knowers are there in the one of you? How many knowers are here? Drop off any misidentification with the body, as was alluded to earlier, and then say how many are here. The entirety of the differentiation vanishes with the elimination of misidentification. Similarly, interiorly, how many knowers are there? Is the mind a secondary consciousness, in addition to the Consciousness of the Self? Are the senses such? Is the ego such? The senses have no light of their own; they shine in reflected light only. You alone are the knower of them, the unseen seer of all that is seen and of all the seeing, the unheard hearer of all that is heard and all of the hearing, and so forth and so on. As for the mind, it also shines by reflected light. The mind consists of ever so many thoughts. Do thoughts know themselves? Can one thought know another thought? Of course not. No matter how many thoughts may appear, there is only one knower of them, and, when the thoughts entirely disappear, that same knower still shines. The knower is not to be defined in terms of the known. It is to be realized conclusively as nonobjective Consciousness.

The only self-effulgent One in myriads of selves. You, the real Self, shine as the Self of all. There is no one who is other. This is the root of supreme peace, and such supreme peace is Bliss. **The Light of the Self will clearly shine within.** When will this happen? It is so as soon as the misidentification subsides. Misidentification is just a vague assumption, an unsupported supposition, a wild hypothesis; it is just false. When the false is known as false, it ceases to exist from that time onward.

This clear illumination of Knowledge, which is supremely blissful, is **the true display of Grace, the ego's death.** Grace may be said to manifest in infinite ways, but it especially shines as true Knowledge, Self-Knowledge, for that alone liberates one from all of the imagined bondage. What is Grace? It is magnificent in its perfection, unlimited in its power, eternal in its duration, and has no cause other that itself. It is always benevolent, revealing that which is the highest good. All one need do is to be keenly aware of it. By such Grace and by such Knowledge, the ego's death is brought about. How do you bring about the death of someone who has never been born? It is by Knowledge of the Truth. If you bring about the ego's death, by the profound inquiry that reveals the self-luminous Consciousness alone to be the Self, you will abide as the Self, and what will be unfolded within you is **the Bliss supreme.**

> In order that the bonds of destiny
> And all its kindred may at last be loosed,
> And so that one may also be released
> From the dread cycle of both birth and death,
> This path than others is far easier;
> Therefore, be still and keep a silent hold
> On tongue and mind and body. That which is
> The self-effulgent will arise within.
> This is the Supreme Experience. Fear will cease.
> This is the boundless sea of perfect Bliss.

The bondage of destiny is said to be produced by one's karma. How is one to be released from the karma and thus from destiny? Unless one is released, the cycle of birth and death, dreaded because of its bondage and suffering, continues, from birth to death and from death to birth. For that which has birth, death is certain; for that which has death, birth is certain; so the Gita proclaims. How is one to be liberated from that? He says **this path,** rather **than others is far easier.** It is easier because it does not assume the existence of the bondage from which one is attempting to become free. Inquiry to know the Self does not assume the various dualisms that one is attempting to transcend. So, it is far easier. It works, and what works must necessarily be easier than that which does not work.

For such release, **be still.** Do not imagine movement in the immovable One. Do not stray away from your Self, in imagination only, thinking of yourself to be this thing and that thing, an ego and a body, with attachment, and so forth and so on. Remain still, with your identity firmly established in its true place. If there is such stillness, if there is identity with the Self and with nothing else, no one remains to have the destiny or to have the karma. If there is no samsari, there is no samsara.

Be still. Remain egoless, free of ignorance, **and keep a silent hold on tongue and mind and body.** In all of your actions, in all of your thinking, and in all of your speaking and communicating, be directed by wisdom and give no scope for the ego. If you would just remain in the Self, as the Self, without the ego arising, how free would you be? "Silence is that in which no "I" appears," Sri Bhagavan has said. This is the silence referred to here. Egoism does not belong anywhere. There is never a good time to be ignorant.

What happens if you practice in this way? **That which is the self-effulgent will arise within.** It will make itself known. All that you need do is remain free of misidentification, and the self-luminous One will shine, Knowledge will be full, wisdom will be natural, and perfect Bliss will shine. **This is the Supreme Experience.** None of this is theoretical. It is all a matter of direct experience. The supreme experience is that in which the triadic difference of experiencer, the experiencing, and the object of experience, is not. They are not divided. Unlike any other kind of experience, it is without beginning and without end.

Fear will cease. An Upanishad declares, "Where there is a second, as it were, there is fear." Where there is a second, someone other than the Self, there is fear. In the absence of a second, in the absence of duality, in the absence of an ego, fearlessness is natural. When all has become the one Self alone, what is there to fear? Fear is always only of another, of something else. No one fears his own Self. He can fear what he regards as himself, but his own Self is fearless and bliss-bestowing. **This is the boundless sea of perfect Bliss.** If you discern that your Being is boundless, such boundless Bliss is also yours. Such perfect Bliss never decays.

> **Annamalai, the Transcendental One,**
> **That is the Eye behind the eye of the mind,**
> **Which eye and other senses cognize[s],**
> **Which in their turn illuminate the sky (space)**
> **And all the other elements as well,**
> **That is again the Spirit-sky (space) in which**
> **The mind-sky (space) does appear; That**
> > **shines within**
> **The Heart which is of every thought quite free**
> **And with gaze fixed within remains fixed as That;**
> **Annamalai (Arunachala), the self-effulgent, shines.**
> **But Grace is needed most. So, faithful be**
> **Unto the Self and Bliss will then result.**

What sees the objects? Your senses. Then, what sees your senses? Your mind. Then, what is that which sees the mind? Beyond the mind, there can be no duality or difference. There is **the Transcendental One.** In what space is this entire manifested universe? It is in the space of the mind. In what space is the mind-space? That is the space of the infinite Consciousness, the space-like Self, the Spirit-space. This immeasurable space **shines within the Heart.** Certainly, the Heart is not small.

Of every thought quite free. Disidentify from thought, cease to view it as existent, and find your perpetual freedom from thought. It never touches you. **And with gaze fixed within remains fixed as That.** To fix your gaze within signifies nonobjective Knowledge. Such should be steady, but because such Knowledge is thought-transcendent, it is not difficult. Remain **as That.** That is Brahman; That is the Self. Tat tvam asi - That you are. Remain as That; who could do otherwise? Inquire. In this way, that which is self-effulgent shines; the self-existent abides.

But Grace is needed most. Grace is always there. Yes, it is needed most, but it is always present. One just has to be keenly aware of it. Where there is Grace, there is no room for the ego and its delusion. Grace is of the Infinite, Grace is of the Eternal; be faithful unto it. Sri Bhagavan said, "Grace is of the Self;" so **faithful be unto the Self.** Cherish That alone, depend on That alone, regard That alone as important, regard That alone as real. You find that which is Grace, that which is the Self, and that which is known as That—Brahman, to be One and the same. **Bliss will then result.** This is a very happy truth; find it within yourself.

In the temple of Being
The space of Consciousness
Om Sri Ramanarpanamastu
Om May this be an offering to Sri Ramana